IDEAS AND TRENDS IN WORLD ANTHROPOLOGY

Xth ICAES SERIES

1. Ideas and Trends in World Anthropology/ Charles Frantz (Ed.)
2. Man and His Environment/ Indera P. Singh and S.C. Tiwari (Eds.)
3. The Communication of Ideas/ J.S. Yadava and Vinayshil Gautam (Eds.)
4. The Tribal World and Its Transformation/ Bhupinder Singh and J. S. Bhandari (Eds.)

About the Editor

CHARLES FRANTZ is currently Professor of Anthropology at the State University of New York, Buffalo, New York, U.S.A. He formerly was the Executive Secretary of the American Anthropological Association, and taught at Howard University, University of Toronto, Portland (Oregon) State University and Ahmadu Bello University (Zaria, Nigeria). He has done fieldwork in Zimbabwe, Nigeria, Cameroun, Canada, and the U.S.A. His publications include *The Student Anthropologist's Handbook, Pastoral Societies, Stratification and National Integration in Africa and Racial Themes in Southern Rhodesia* (co-authored with Cyril A. Rogers). His current interests are in the history and profession of anthropology, pastoralist societies, intercultural relations, and theory.

Xth ICAES SERIES NO. 4
General Editor : LALITA P. VIDYARTHI

IDEAS AND TRENDS IN WORLD ANTHROPOLOGY

Edited by
CHARLES FRANTZ

CONCEPT PUBLISHING COMPANY PVT. LTD.
NEW DELHI-110059

ISBN: 978-81-7022-183-8

Edition 2023

Published and Printed by

Concept
Since 1974

Concept Publishing Company Pvt. Ltd.
A/15-16, Commercial Block, Mohan Garden,
New Delhi-110059 (India)
T : 91-11-41101460
E : publishing@conceptpub.com, *W*: www.conceptpub.com

GENERAL EDITOR'S INTRODUCTION

THE International Congress of Anthropological and Ethnological Sciences (ICAES) has been meeting at intervals since the year 1934 excluding, of course, the World War II years. It has however, taken forty-four long years before the venue could be shifted to a Third World country. The time gap is significant and indicates the general trend of the growth of the discipline.

Anthropology was once considered a tool for discovering the relative practices and customs of peoples who were destined to be governed, and thereby at best to be discovered in order to serve the purpose of the superior, the "civilised" industrialised nations. Very often the study of such peoples also provided insights to help in sound colonial administration. Physical anthropology, besides tracing the ascent of man, was used at times to find out if there was indeed a fundamental difference between the races. As a result of all this activity much data was recorded and the scientists of the industrial urban cultures of Europe and America became aware of the less developed half of the world. Whether this meant real advancement of scientific knowledge in all such cases may be open to question; for that matter, it may even cause one to wonder about the meaning and quality of the cultural encounter of the colonial period. This is bound to be very different from exchanges between groups of people who respect each other. Such an encounter between equals would perhaps have provided a lasting base both for understanding and for an enduring relationship. But as the pattern of anthropological investigation emerged in such exploitative contexts, apparently plausible sets of reasons were given to discredit anthropological inquiry of this kind.

World War II, however, proved to be catalytic in the changes that it effected in the "science of man". Its repercussions were many and widespread. The post-war years heralded the disintegration of the colonial empires and with it a transformation in the attitude towards those who had hitherto been under the colonial yoke. On another plane speedier modes of travel and communication and other significant advances in technology have brought the peoples of the world closer to each other.

More and more international gatherings have opened up new vistas of research and study. Each nation has applied the motto : *know thyself*, while attempting to project its image abroad. The vision is no longer constricted; the analyses no longer partial. This localization and internationalization have stimulated the formulation of theories and working models in the social sciences; the anthropological and ethnological sciences are the foremost among these sciences to have set the trend. The results have been spectacular : witness the success of the ten congresses held all over the world up to 1978.

It is but fitting that the first of the congresses to be held in the Third World countries should have been held in India. This country was perhaps the earliest to shake off the yoke of colonialism and blaze the trail of independence.

I have maintained elsewhere that up to a point the history of the congresses is the history of the growth of anthropology. Accordingly I have periodised the congresses in the following manner : *Institutionalisation* : *The Early Phase* : the London Congress (1934), the Copenhagen Congress (1938); *Anthropology in a World Reborn* : the Brussels Congress (1948); *The Age of Consolidation* : the Vienna Congress (1952), the Philadelphia Congress (1956), the Paris Congress (1960); *Towards a Richer Mix* : the Moscow Congress (1964), the Tokyo Congress (1968), the Chicago Congress (1973); *The Third World Orientation* : the Delhi Congress (1978).*

The 1978 Congress in Delhi provided an opportunity to survey the terrain of anthropology from a different vantage point. Two things emerged very clearly from the papers presented at the various sessions. One, that the nature of data available as a result of anthropological studies was copious and abundant but very often unrelated. Little sustained effort has been made to read and study them in a fashion which

* For details please refer to L.P. Vidyarthi : *The Rise of World Anthropology*, New Delhi : Concept Publishing Company (1979).

would lead to the deciphering of meaningful patterns. The second was the reinforcement at a specific level of a view which many hold but is rarely so well brought out, viz; anthropology as a science of man being the most pervading and all embracing. Sessions during the Congress ranged from linguistics to management, from tribes to industrial cultures. Several levels of researches on the physical evolution of man in diverse environmental settings were reported.

While it is accepted that international conferences play a vital role in the dissemination of ideas and information and provide a forum for the exchange of such views, the printed word has a far wider impact and reaches a larger audience. Necessarily therefore, its utility is far greater and more lasting. Hence the publication of the papers presented at the Xth ICAES assumes great importance. The fact that their publications is being undertaken in this country is doubly significant. It is in many ways symbolic of the change that has come about in the sciences themselves.

Motivated by the urge to place this wealth of material before a wider audience we have taken upon ourselves the task of editing and publishing the various papers presented during the Congress. The point of the whole exercise is to collate much valuable research effort, and by this endeavour to achieve a normative upgrading of the status of research in the world of anthropology, thus contributing our mite to the summum bonum of human knowledge.

As one surveys the scene at the commencement of the last two decades of this century it seems increasingly clear that whereas symbolic anthropology and psycho-social inter-face studies shall continue to be made, the anthropology of the future would be broader and deeper in context than it has been so far. Beyond the searches for epistemology, analysis of bio-social interface, genetic studies, analysis of symbology, networks and strategic problems in culture history, shall emerge a richer anthropology which might serve as the integration of much information, analysis and insight. There is an urgent need to bring this about keeping in view the needs of a threatened human ecology, a rapidly deteriorating energy situation, an increasing consideration for the sub-cultures of various nationalities, growing substitutes involved in optimising natural, financial and human resources and thereby managing development.

It is our hope that the volumes in this series shall make some contribution towards the emergence of a more integrated growth of anthropology as the real science of man. The strength of this area of activity is really the combined strength of a whole range of other disciplines all of which relate to the study of some aspect of man. Accordingly the series shall be very comprehensive. This alone shall reflect that the Delhi Congress was able to achieve a high water-mark in anthropological studies which many believed would serve as a trend setter for the future.

The delegates to the Xth ICAES were nearly 3500 representing 63 countries. The participants contributed about 1000 papers covering a wide range of topics.

Our task here has been merely to collate the mass of material and present it in a series of handy readable volumes. Posterity shall be the judge of its merits as it shall be the chief user of its content. The groupings of the papers in each volume have been done in a vaguely discernible pattern so as to make each one independent of the other. The whole series, however, presents itself as a record of a period in the history of human society.

By providing wider perspectives and deeper insights, this voluminous project should secure the foundations for a meaningful study of man which will help in reducing disparities among peoples and imbalances in the development of societies.

We are not unaware of the challenging nature of the task before us in undertaking to publish this series of volumes. The success of this venture will depend ultimately on the efforts of all those interested in anthropological studies. That the International Council for Philosophy and Humanistic Studies has provided the initial grant for the first three volumes and a partial grant for this volume in order to commence the publication project is certainly a heartening indication of this interest.

This volume is devoted entirely to ideas and trends in world anthropology. Papers have been selected from those presented at some of the sessions of the Congress or at symposia held at the time which bring out very clearly the theoretical aspects in anthropological studies and the ideas that have emerged for discussion thus marking the trends that can be observed in such studies from the global perspective. Veering away from the "Americanization" of the early days, the papers in this volume show that there has been a perceptible development towards a synthetic approach to the study of anthropology. In forging a synthesis between Western and non-Western modes of thought and conceptualization, anthropology today is evolving into a truly international discipline which augurs well for its future as the Science of Man.

We are extremely happy that Concept Publishing Company have undertaken the arduous task of bringing out these volumes. We are confident that they will complete the entire project both efficiently and expeditiously.

We would like to say a word of thanks to Professor Charles Frantz for the painstaking editing of this volume single handed.

We also acknowledge here our gratitude to Professor Surjit C. Sinha for permitting us to include in this volume several papers read at a session of which he was Co-Chairman.

One word more in conclusion : The views expressed in these volumes are not necessarily those of the editors or the ICAES. The responsibility for them rests solely with the contributors.

Ranchi University
Ranchi, Bihar,
India
March, 1981

LALITA P. VIDYARTHI
President
Xth ICAES &
IUAES (1973-78)

INTRODUCTION

On Paradigms and their Application

ANTHROPOLOGY has become significantly more internationalized during the past few decades (Freedman 1977, Vidyarthi 1979b). This was demonstrated forcefully when the 9th International Congress of Anthropological and Ethnological Sciences met in Chicago in 1973. Those meetings were noticeably marked by significant increases in (a) the number of participants from the less industrialized nations of the world, and (b) concerns about numerous philosophical, scientific, methodological, and political aspects of anthropological and ethnological disciplines (Vidyarthi 1979a, Huizer and Mannheim 1979). Both before and after the Chicago meetings, however, a growing number of books and articles have been published concerning the content, organization, and problematics of anthropology (e.g., Harris 1968, Hymes 1969, Tenneke 1971, Copans 1971, 1974, Gulian 1973, Asad 1973, Hsu 1973, Bauman 1973, Voget 1975, Frank 1975, Honigmann 1976, Wallace *et al.* 1977, Shimkin *et al.* 1978, Fahim and Helmer 1980).

It was within that dynamic context that a symposium on the main ideas and trends in anthropology was conceived. Letters of invitation were sent to dozens of scholars, but most were either unable to attend or had committed themselves to read papers at other sessions in New Delhi. The contributions in this volume thus are of mixed origin: Six of the papers were read at the symposium, chaired by Prof. Surjit C. Sinha and myself, whereas the others were presented in different sessions. Noteworthy among the latter is the address given by Prof. Vidyarthi, President of the Xth International Congress.

Substantively, the papers in this volume fall into two loose categories. One set concerns socio-cultural anthropology and the wider society, particularly in relation to development programs. The second set examines selected aspects of development within the disciplines. It is apparent that the papers neither cover all regions and nations of the world nor many newer subfields and paradigms, such as exchange, dependency, systems, centre-periphery, and biogenetic theories, or the emergent areas of anthropology concerned with health, urban communities, legal systems, warfare, and so forth. I know of no single-authored volume which comprehensively covers, let alone synthesizes, all these problematics (cf. Frantz 1977a, 1977b), although some multi-authored works (e.g., Poirier 1966, Honigmann 1977, and the *Annual Reviews of Anthropology*) are exceptionally useful in helping to approach that goal. In order to attain anything like a full coverage of ideas and trends in world anthropology, it will be necessary to consult other volumes, now being published, which contain papers read at the Xth International Congress.

Paradigmatic Trends

Anthropologists today are working in gardens with a hundred flowering paradigms. Vidyarthi, in his paper, speaks of the post-Second World War period as one in which anthropology has become "Americanized" (see also Vidyarthi 1975, 1979a, 1979b). One main characteristic of the discipline in the U.S.A. is a recognition of the organizational and intellectual value of trying to keep together diverse disciplines which focus on prehistory and archaeology, ethnology, social anthropology linguistics, and physical or biological anthropology. This vision and organization closely parallel those of the International Congress and the International Union of Anthropological and Ethnological Sciences. Among the reasons for the spread of the U.S.A. version of anthropology may have been its diversification of paradigms and efforts to synthesize them; but, in addition, there have been other important factors : The worldwide spread of English as a medium of communication; the U.S.A.'s increased political, economic, scientific, and technological ascendency; and its having a disproportionate number of anthropological teachers, researchers, funds, and institutions.

The progressive development in applying anthropology around the world also owes much to the strengths of the U.S.A. in pragmatic philosophy, Protestant values, and mercantile capitalism, although the genesis of such efforts was probably in Great Britain and, to a lesser extent, other colonial powers. Much of U.S.A. anthropology's interest in the application of its knowledge seems to have derived from its close association in universities with sociology, the latter being more concerned with (albeit generally non-Western) social programs and reforms. In the U.S.A., anthropology became more involved with the social sciences after 1920, and social and cultural anthropology grew more quickly than did archaeology and physical or biological anthropology. One evidence of this is suggested in Frantz's paper concerning the special fields of competence of persons elected to the presidency of the American Anthropological Association since the time of its inception.

Zubrow's paper discusses a variant of U.S.A. (and British) influence in other nations by examining periodical literature to ascertain the spread of a relatively recent and more deductive theoretical paradigm in archaeology. Sarker's contribution also documents how U.S. American conceptions of anthropology are affecting the development of teaching and research in Bangladesh. One might go on to demonstrate the manner and degree of U.S.A. influence upon anthropology elsewhere (cf. Freedman 1977, Frank 1975, Vidyarthi 1979b), but this could easily lead to overlooking the many non-American influences which have contributed to the internationalization of anthropology and ethnology.

The world development of anthropology continues to be influenced by ideas and paradigms that were initially formulated by scholars in several other nations. Not only can one point to the continuing influence of Darwin, Lamarck, Marx, Kropotkin, Frobenius, Freud, Durkheim, Mauss, Weber, Radcliffe-Brown, Malinowski, and others; there also has been an abiding international interest in the ideas of Lévi-Strauss, Piaget, Firth, Fortes, Evans-Pritchard, Gluckman, Barth, Godelier, Meillassoux, Ribiero, Leach, Dumont, Srinivas, Goody, and Bailey, among others. Overall, the most internationally followed paradigms in anthropology are those which assume that human life is shaped mainly by either subconscious or unconscious "structures" (e.g., Marx, Freud, Radcliffe Brown, Piaget, and Lévi-Strauss), and all these have been formulated by non-Americans. Littleton's paper discusses the universality (species-wise) of mental/cognitive structures postulated by Lévi-Strauss, and contrasts this with Dumézil's formulation that such structures are attributes of historically related cultural groups (especially language families, e.g., Indo-European, Uto-Aztecan, and ancient Semitic). Other scholars, on the other hand, hold that ideological, cognitive, logical, or ideational "structures" are more ethnic or culture-specific, or even unique to individuals, and furthermore that they are not necessarily static through the course of one's life (cf. Kapferer 1976, Maruyama 1980, Fahim and Helmer 1980).

The potential for generating new or modifying existing paradigms in anthropology is enormous. Mauroof, in his paper, suggests some lines of development that are possible if Islamic conceptions or paradigms were utilized. Vidyarthi also refers to some formulations in Hindu thought, as well as to Gandhi, that may invigorate anthropology. In the paper by Das, he cites Acharya B.N. Seal's *Positive Sciences of the Ancient Hindus* (1915), which suggests another bountiful type of resource for future cross-paradigmatic growth. An even richer anthropology may be anticipated as paradigms contained within Chinese, Indonesian, Persian, Navajo, Quechua, Maori, and dozens of other systems of thought enter into international anthropology.

Finally, it is worth emphasizing a point made by Mauroof, Vidyarthi, Mandelbaum, and Charsley : Our paradigms today are much less focused on small-scale and/or presumptively isolated units, such as tribes and communities. The "island mentality" of most structural-functional anthropologists by default left the study of "peasants," urban systems, "civilizations," and radical social and cultural change and conflict to specialists who called themselves Orientalists, Sinologists, Islamicists, and Sociologists (cf. Redfield 1956). Since World War II, with the development and spread of new paradigms in anthropology, perhaps most of all Marxian ones, this is no longer as true. Meanwhile, paradigmatic changes in anthropology have been accompanied by the growing international use of mathematics, statistics, and computers to analyze data, a point illustrated in Zubrow's discourse.

Trends in the Uses of Anthropology

A second focus of many contributors to this volume concerns the relationship of anthropology to the wider world, and more specifically to development programs. In earlier decades, the most practical uses of socio-cultural authropology were to help governments deal with ethnic monorities, and with disadvantaged, poor, or powerless groups and individuals within their own boundaries or in colonial and trust territories. Much of this activity was an outgrowth (either showing continuity or regeneration) of earlier Eurocentric concerns with progress, religious conversion, increased productivity and trade, and the spread of literacy, rationalism, and science (cf. Colson 1976). Das's paper serves, however, to correct a widespread bias that all conceptions and programs for progress or development originated in Europe. He describes many of the diligent and imaginative activities of a leading Indian scholar, Acharya Brajendra Nath Seal, who actively strove to reduce violence, war, and casteism, and alternatively to generate better living standards, peace, and harmony across racial, cultural, caste, class, and nationality lines.

Today, adorned with new labels of reform or development, an elastic but inter-related set of values and goals has become integral to almost every nation as it endeavors to modify old or generate new social and cultural systems. In the last few decades anthropology has become increasingly involved in programs of change and development, but in two different ways, as Charsley indicates. One mode of articulation has been through what he calls the "anthropology of development," an open-minded study of changing social systems, without personal involvement by the investigator. The other approach he terms "development anthropology," in which professionals are actively engaged in *praxis* (thought plus action). His own paper, which discusses the problematics of being a local agricultural change agent, is an example of the richness of the latter approach.

Since the theme of the Xth International Congress in New Delhi was "Anthropology and the Challenges of Development",

Vidyarthi's and Mandelbaum's keynote addresses are significant statements about the present and potential future relationship of anthropology to the wider world. The influences of world political and economic crises during the last century, together with the "social scientizing" of anthropology and the spread of transformational and revolutionary ideologies, has brought an increased concern and involvement of anthropologists in designing, implementing, and evaluating programs of change, including development. Mandelbaum asks whether anthropology has something unique to offer in such efforts, and his answer is in the affirmative. He points to anthropology's heavy emphasis on holism, contextualism and participant observation, as well as its serious effort to both comprehend and respect endogenous knowledge. Anthropologists, in other words, are more likely than other development specialists to be interested in the quality of life, in contrast to, say, the gross national product. Vidyarthi makes a similar point in discussing the views of Gandhi ond other Indian thinkers, suggesting the value of non-Western paradigms for changing, developing, and studying or evaluating social systems. It seems correct to say that, compared to many scholars in other disciplines, anthropologists are more inclined to recognize the existence of multiple paths to development, happiness, and the fulfilment of aspirations.

While anthropologists seem less likely than other social and humanistic scholars to have ethnocentric and Eurocentric biases about progress or development, this is not universally true. Many scholars and activists hold contrary views, for example, "vulgar materialists" and evangelical Christian missionaries who favor or propagandize unilineal views and extraneously generated programs. Lombard, in his contribution, says that one of the two major concerns within contemporary French socio-cultural anthropology is about the development or transformation of economic and social structures, in order to reduce or eliminate inequities in power, wealth, and status. A similar concern has developed among anthropologists in most other nations as well, perhaps most of all in the less wealthy and industrialized ones. There is little conclusive evidence at present, however, to suggest that any ideological system is inimical to different modes of development, whether it be Hinduism (Vidyarthi's chapter), Islam (Dia 1975), Christianity

(Wilson 1971, Salamone 1979), or some other system. The most general anthropological view with respect to development seems to parallel that about the discipline itself : Let a hundred flowers bloom and new ones be constantly generated (cf. Jantsch 1975).

Conclusion

The symposium on ideas and trends in world anthropology was a modest but important one. It touched upon several of the major changes in the paradigms used by contemporary anthropologists, as well as their varieties of involvement in programs designed to benefit humankind. A significant division remains today in the anthropological and ethnological sciences, however : Some aver they have discovered "God's truth" or "history's truths" ("scientific laws"), while others are more eclectic or relativistic, either by conviction or experience. The latter group seems to encourage the continuation of a multi-paradigmatic discipline, as well as following multiple routes to, or types of, development. Since the latter group seems to be more consonant with the nature of human socio-cultural systems, they are more likely than scientistic and or deterministic paradigmatists to shape anthropological ideas and trends in the future.

Department of Anthropology, CHARLES FRANTZ
State University of New York, Buffalo
New York, U.S.A.
10 February 1981

SUGGESTED READINGS

Asad, T., (ed.), *Anthropology and the Colonial Encounter*. London : Ithaca Press, 1973.

Bauman, Z., *Culture as Praxis*. London : Routledge and Kegan Paul, 1973.

Colson, E., "Culture and Progress". *American Anthropologist* 78, 1976, 261-171.

Copans, J., Godelier, M., Tornay, S., et Backès-Clément, C., *L'anthropologie : Sciences des sociétés primitives? (La point de la question, v. 8)*. Paris : Éditions E. P. 1971.

Copans, J., *Critiques et politiques de l'anthropologie.* Paris : F. Maspero, 1974.

Dia, M., Islam : *Sociétés Africaines et culture industrielle.* Dakar : Les Nouvelles Éditions Africaines, 1975.

Fahim, H., and Helmer, K., "Indigenous Anthropology in Non-Western Countries : A Further Elaboration". *Current Anthropology* 21, 1980, 644-650.

Frank, A. G., "Anthropology—Ideology, Applied Anthropology—Politics". *Race and Class* 17, 1975, 51-68.

Frantz, C., "Review of F. W. Voget : A History of Ethnology". *American Anthropologist* 79, 1977a, 447-449.

——, Review of J. J. Honigmann, "The Development of Anthropological Ideas". *Reviews in Anthropology* 5 (1), 1977b, 25-33.

Freedman, M., "Social and Cultural Anthropology." In Havet, J., (ed), *Main Trends in the Social and Human Sciences.* Paris and The Hague : Mouton/UNESCO, Pt. 2, v. 1 : 1977, 3-176.

Gulian, C., *Versuch einer marxistischen philosophischen Anthropologie.* Darmstadt : Luchterhand, 1973.

Harris, M., *The Rise of Anthropological Theory.* New York : Thomas Y. Crowell, 1968.

Honigmann, J.J., (ed.), *Handbook of Social and Cultural Anthropology.* Chicago : Rand McNally, 1973.

Honigmann, J. J., *The Development of Anthropological Ideas.* Homewood. Ill. : Dorsey Press, 1976.

Hsu, F. L. K., "Prejudice and its Intellectual Effect in American Anthropology : An Ethnographic Report." *American Anthropologist* 75, 1973, 1-19.

Huizer, G., and Mannheim, B. (eds.), *The Politics of Anthropology.* The Hague : Mouton, 1979.

Hymes, D. H., (ed.), *Reinventing Anthropology.* New York : Random House, 1969.

Jantsch, E., *Design for Evolution : Self-Organization and Planning in the Life of Human System.* New York : George Braziller, 1975.

Kapferer, B., (ed.), *Transaction and Meaning.* Philadelphia : Institute for the Study of Human Issues, 1976.

Maruyam, M., "Mindscapes and Scientific Theories." *Current Anthropology,* 21, 1980, 589-599, 607-608.

Poirier, J. (ed.), "Ethnologie générale" (Encyclopédie de la Pléiade, v. 24). Paris : Éditions Gallimard, 1966.

Redfield, R., *Peasant Society and Culture : An Anthropological Approach to Civilization.* Chicago : University of Chicago Press, 1956.

Salamone, F. A., "Epistemological Implications of Fieldwork and their Consequences". *American Anthropologist* 81, 1979, 46-60.

Shimkin, D. B., Tax. S., and Morrison, J. W., (eds.), "Anthropology for the Future" (Research Reports, no. 4) Urbana. Ill.: Department of Anthropology, University of Illinois, 1978,

Tennekes, J., *Anthropology : Relativism and Method : An Inquiry into the Methodological Principles of a Science of Culture.* Assen : Van Gorcum, 1971.

Vidyarthi, L. P., "The Rise of Social Anthropology in India (1774-1972) : A Historical Appraisal." In Thoresen, T. H. H., (ed.) *Toward a Science of Man : Essays in the History of Anthropology.* The Hague : Mouton, 1975, pp. 159-182.

——, *Rise of World Anthropology as Reflected through the International Congresses (1934-1978).* New Delhi : Concept Publishing Company, 1979a.

——. *Trends in World Anthropology.* New Delhi : Concept Publishing Company, 1979b.

Voget, F. W., *A History of Ethnology.* New York : Holt, Rinehart, and Winston, 1975.

Wallace, A. F. C., *et al.*, (eds.), *Perspectives on Anthropology.* Washington, D. C.: American Anthropological Association (Special Publications, no. 10), 1977.

Wilson, M., *Religion and the Transformation of Society : A Study in Social Change in Africa.* Cambridge, Eng. : Cambridge University Press, 1971.

CONTENTS

LIST OF CONTRIBUTORS

S.R. Charsley

University of Glasgow, U.K.

Trilochan Das

B-1/20, Hauz Khas, New Delhi - 110016.
(Member, Authors Guild of India, New Delhi)

Charles Frantz

Professor, Department of Anthropology,
State University of New York, Buffalo
New York, U.S.A.

Jacques Lombard

Professor, Université des Sciences et Techniques
de Lille, France

David G. Mandelbaum

Professor, Department of Anthropology,
University of California, Berkeley, U.S.A.

Mohammed Mauroof

Department of Social and Behavioral Sciences,
Cheyney State College, Cheyney, U.S.A.

Profulla C. Sarker

Assistant Professor, Department of Social Work,
University of Rajshahi, Bangladesh

C. Scott Littleton

Occidental College, Los Angeles,
California, U.S.A.

L.P. Vidyarthi

Professor and Head, Department of
Anthropology, University of Ranchi, Bihar

Ezra B.W. Zubrow

Department of Anthropology, State University of
New York, Buffalo, New York, U.S.A.

ONE

L.P. Vidyarthi

TRENDS IN WORLD ANTHROPOLOGY*

I FEEL a sense of honour and deep personal satisfaction in welcoming you to this country with consummate tradition and a past full of cultural achievements. Here social diversity forms a cultural mosaic. Even though life in India has a refinement displaying several levels of socio-cultural and economic developments, the pulsations are essentially one. As a part of the presidential endeavour, I propose to present the contemporary theme of World Anthropology in a historical perspective as has emerged from the last nine International Congresses (1934-78).[1] While doing so, I shall touch upon the possible future trends of World Anthropology.

Anthropology, the Science of Man has been on the march through the ages. The twentieth century witnessed the institutionalisation of anthropology at a global level. It was left to the British anthropologists to take the initiative in organising the First International Congress of 1934, in London. By that time, the traditional concepts of Social Evolution and Diffusion were being discarded in favour of the British Structural-Functional School.[2] This formative phase of institutionalisation of anthropology, further strengthened the British social anthropology and created a climate in its favour during the Second International Congress, held at Copenhagen in 1938. However, during the Second World War, anthropology sustained a great set-back and needed to be revitalised.

* The Presidential address from the International Congress of Anthropological and Ethnological Sciences, New Delhi, 1978.

When the Third International Congress met at Brussels in 1948, the Science of Man was reborn after the ravages of the Second World War. The Fourth International Congress at Vienna in 1952 opened new areas of research and created a climate for the consolidation and expansion of the discipline.

The United States of America hosted the Congress for the first time, when its Fifth Session was held at Philadelphia in 1956. Viewed in the backdrop of 1952 International Symposium of Anthropology under the Chairmanship of A.L. Kroeber, the Philadelphia Congress amply demonstrated the post-war dominance of American anthropology throughout the world. This meeting was marked by the participation of a greater number of scholars from different parts of the world and included delegates from the USSR who attended this Congress for the first time.

The picture of anthropology and the methodological approach conceived for study of the "integrated man" that emerged from the 1952 International Symposium dominated the planning and deliberation of the Fifth International Congress. This also influenced the publication of the widely circulated book, *Current Anthropology* (Thomas 1956), followed by the regular publication of *Current Anthropology*, which continued to publish papers from all over the world on Pre-history, Archaeology, Linguistics, Folklore, Ethnology, Social Anthropology, and Physical Anthropology. Anthropological enquiries at the international level continued to be dominated by the above approach. Even the Sixth International Congress held at Paris in 1960 continued to be influenced by this approach where the structural-functional school had its moorings including the influence of Levi-Strauss.

The ground for a richer mix of theoretical concepts and methodological approach was under preparation when the Seventh, Eighth and Ninth International Congresses met at Moscow (1964), Tokyo-Kyoto (1968), and Chicago (1973) respectively. These sessions reflected the closer interactions of ideas, concepts, and theories. The Soviet ethnography developed on the ideologies of Marx, Engels and Lenin marked the revival of the concept of social evolution. This added a new dimension to anthropology, made it more balanced, and marginally reduced the Anglo-American influence.[3] Such a revival, reinterpretation, and recognition of neo-evolutionism to analyse and understand the class societies was a significant development in the contemporary anthropological theories. This was a pointer to a greater mix and a wider horizon for the forthcoming anthropological researches.

The development of anthropological theories show that the previous quarter of the century has been the most productive period in the history of World Anthropology. We have also witnessed an accelerated proliferation and diversification of the sub-fields in anthropology. The juxtapositioning of the earlier theories and methods alongwith the newer ones further contributed to the expansive nature of anthropology. In its expansion, inter-disciplinarity, and choice of topics the only limiting factor was Man. In view of these developments, anthropology was designated as a revolutionary discipline ; "a modern metaphysics, a science of sciences that may enquire into the nature of history and man for the sake of man and in his name" (Diamond 1964 : 433). To some, the extent of proliferation was a matter of concern lest it brought about the extinction of anthropology itself. Such a fear for others, was unfounded, since eclecticism has remained the basic strength of anthropology.

The period under review is also noted for the independence of the European colonies and the consequent increase of contacts with America. This accelerated the post-war shift from the colonial climate of European anthropology to that of American anthropology. The smooth transition was also attributed to America's increasing utilisation of its great resources, discovery of new techniques of research, theoretical models, and above all, its effective use of diverse media of communication.

In the process, American anthropology acquired the undisputed leadership in the discipline. This monopolistic situation continued unabated through the mid-sixties. The over Americanisation of the theory, methods, and field expeditions were resented, as on occasion, it fell short in explaining the complexities of the traditional societies of India, Japan, and South-East Asia. To some, the Americanisation was so overwhelming that it was considered a switchover from colonial to neo-colonial anthropology. A variety of reactions were expressed about the over Americanisation of anthropology. Loubser views the situation in terms of the vertical relationship between the social scientists of Europe and North America, and those of the Third World. This implies the intellectual imperialism and colonial exploitation (Loubser 1977). Bose while making a plea for the decolonisation of Indian anthropology, commented that ; "the position of Indian Anthropology has, on the whole, been colonial in relation to schools which have dominated the European or American scene from time to time" (Bose 1963 : 46). Gore refers to this ambivalence and observes that it hinges not only upon our approach to American social sciences but on nearly everything American. Other criticism of American scholars is based on an assumption of superficiality, inadequate field work, and indiscriminate application of questionnaire as a tool for data collection (Gore : N.D.). Those who have found American influence beneficial indicated the growing sophistication of research methodology, the use of new terms and concepts in analysis, the diversification of research interest, and the introduction, adoption, and spread of theoretical models.

A few scholars trained in America complained that, "many of us still publish to gain approvals from our patrons and mentors in the West" (Sarana and Sinha 1976 : 219). Another scholar expressed the need to enquire into the extent of academic patronage which has continued to be a decisive factor in shaping the contour of scholarly enterprise in anthropology in India today (Sinha 1971).

Similarly, in the light of the Japanese experience, Nakane finds the application of the Western model inadequate for the understanding of Japanese society. She refers to the disservice done even by the Japanese sociologists "who disposed of their indigenous phenomena that did not fit western theories precisely by labelling them as Japan's 'feudal' or 'backward' elements a very convenient solution and the general public readily accepted this explanation" (Nakane 1972 : 2).

In the light of his experience of South East Asia, Alatas wrote about the dependence of developing countries on western scholarship. He has systematically established that western colonialism in the developing societies has created a class of imitative intellectuals or "captive minds"—a stage of intellectual bondage and a dependence or external groups through the operation of such media as ; books, institutions' radio, press, television, conferences, and meetings (Alatas 1974).

Although there is a general reaction against uncritical imitation, the western method of analysis is not to be entirely shunned but, rather, to be selectively integrated with the indigenous modes. There is a need to separate the universal aspects of anthropological theories and methods from their particular associations with the West. After identifying the concepts applicable to India, Japan, South-East Asia or elsewhere, we may consider which of their specific aspects could be modified in relation to the regions where they are to be used. The national and historical settings will help to make it effective, organic, and relevant.

In the light of my own research experience, I have found many of the European and American concepts, theories, and methods to be inapplicable to Indian society. These limitations hinder the understanding of the complexities of Indian society and culture. It was under such an awareness and experience that I proposed the need for Indianness in social sciences, even other than anthropology, as early as 1964.[4]

India has a rich tradition of social thinkers with an intimate understanding of social issues. This has brought about socio-cultural transformations. This reminds me of an observation made by Jayaprakash Narayan—referring to the explorations made to-date on the writings of Mahatma Gandhi as being inadequate and suggested that there was a much larger "Submerged part of the iceberg".[5]

To consider just one of Gandhiji's significant contributions, we could refer to his approach to tribal culture. About this Gandhiji wrote profusely. In 1942 he wrote; "Anyway no one who hopes to construct *Swaraj* on the foundations of non-violence can afford to neglect even the least of India's sons—*Adivasis* too numerous to be counted among the least". (Gandhi 1942). Gandhiji devoted some of his valuable time to the problems of the tribes and of the *Hrijans* (considered to be untouchable and backward). He was perhaps the first Indian of this century to recognise that a society whose foundations were weak cannot last long. The erosion from beneath will eat away the whole superstructure of the society. This called for immediate rectification. Though the Gandhian approach to the neglected tribals was basically humanitarian, his philosophy was practical and best suited to the tribal conditions.

Gandhiji felt that even the dissenting tribals of the frontier regions were amenable to reason and advised; "If I had my way I would go and mix with them and argue it out with them, and I am sure they cannot be impervious to the argument of love and reason" (Tendulkar 1954 : 360-361).

He firmly believed that the tribal religion was in no way different from formal Hinduism. He disapproved of the conversion of the tribals to an alien faith motivated by material inducements. For this he prescribed, "Reform from Within" and advised the *Savarna* (the twice-born) to be in selfless service to these depressed people (Gandhi 1936).

It is easy to see that the Gandhian Philosophy of tribal transformation still holds great relevance in the present day context. It is for the Indian anthropologists to take them seriously and not to be carried away by the voluminous writings of the western scholars who termed them to be "animist", "savages" and very different from the Hindus.

In the field of social sciences, the writings of Sri Aurobindo and Rabindranath Tagore are equally rich. If Gandhiji attempted to establish the oneness of mankind in terms of non-violence and talked of establishing a sort of spiritual humanism, Sri Aurobindo discussed at length the cosmic evolution. His thoughts are based on higher levels of spiritual consciousness (Srivastava 1968). Rabindranath Tagore through his writings reflected on the problems of rural India at a human and spiritual level. He also gained experience through his experiment of rural reconstruction among the tribal and folk villages of Bengal, and even today the Institute of Rural Development founded him reminds us of his pioneering efforts in this field.[6] These and other social thinkers like Raja Ram Mohan Roy, Vinoba Bhave, Vivekananda, Jayaprakash Narayan, M.N. Roy, Dada Dharmadhikari, Ram Manohar Lohia, Ishwar Chandra Vidyasagar, Bhudev Mukhopadhyay, Benoy Sarkar, Lokmanya Bal Gangadhar Tilak, etc., are so different from the western scholars. Their works should not be ignored by social scientists who wish to understand the Indian society and culture.

Darwin considered Man as an integral part of the animal kingdom and Freud joined him to assert that man's thought and behaviour are conditioned primarily by the libido, i.e., sex. Marx in a similar vein rejected all spiritual values and laid stress on the material and economic well-being of humanity. These western thinkers are radically different from Gandhiji, Aurobindo, Tagore, and others who thought of man and his society in terms of spiritual humanism, universal love, and non-violence. These are positive approaches and any occidental bias should not be permitted to taint our social sciences with a fragmented and slanted picture. In order to introduce Indianness in social sciences, there is a dire need to give due emphasis to the writings of the earlier and contemporary social thinkers.

Again, in a historical context, India's ancient scriptures like the *Vedas*, the *Upanishads* the *Smriti*, the *Puranas*, and the *Epics* provide a sensitive insight into the social realities. These ancient scriptures reflect the wisdom and provide guidelines for shaping the socio-cultural life in India. The patterns of nature-man relationship, man to man relationship, and man to spirit relationship are explained in great depth. The basic elements of the Indian life-style lie in their traditional practice of four-fold *Ashramas*, four-fold *Purusarthas*, the sixteen *Sanskaras*, etc., which still continue to influence the ethos, world view, and the life of an average Indian.

The Indianness in social science has to emerge with a proper appraisal of these ancient texts whose influences on the behavioural pattern of our countrymen cannot be neglected. There is a case for evolving the concepts of applied historical anthropology.

At this stage, I would like to comment on the attitude of the western scholars towards the dominance of religion on the thinking and practice of Indian social thinkers and Indian people. Myrdal, for example, stresses the negative influences of religion as practised in Asia (including India). He goes on to criticise the Indian religious reformers who, according to him, suggest and work for reform under "western influence", but attempt to find support for their ideals in Hindu scriptures from the times of the *Vedas*. He says :

Among masses, these traditional beliefs that with their

> related valuations have religious sanction are normally irrational, for they are superstitious and imply a mystical rather than a logical way of thinking. Religious conceptions, to that degree irrational, have not commonly been held in the West for centuries. To a considerable lesser extent, irrational beliefs sanctioned by religion are also present among the educated class including its intellectual elite (Myrdal 1968 : 78).

At yet another place, he makes a sweeping statement and calls religion entirely useless :

> Understood in this realistic and comprehensive sense, religion usually acts as a tremendous force for social inertia. The writer knows no instance in present day South Asia where religion has induced social change (Myrdal 1968 : 104).

Apparently, Myrdal has a negative attitude towards the potential function of religious reform. His attitude inclines towards the uprooting and undermining of the Asian religious traditions.

While time does not permit me a detailed deliberation on this issue, to my mind, Myrdal's view on religion is extremely exclusive and his treatment of Asian religion is biased. He has exaggerated the negative influence of religion on development.

With India's style of life, "*Dharma* (wrongly translated into religion) is the first of the four fundamental principles of social ethics for man in the form of "*Purushartha*". The word literally means : 'the meaning of man' or 'the aim of being human'. The other three principles are : *Artha* (wealth), *Kama* (desire), and *Moksha* (salvation). It is man's duty to fulfil the first three, in order of priority and live with purity to achieve the last. In this manner, it is clear that with regard to the aims of human life, an Indian emphasises an integral approach to development and deserves to be interpreted in the proper context.[7]

I shall end the address with one more observation relating to the nature of research that the scholars of the Third World should undertake. In the course of his review of scientific developments in the new states, Edward Shils classified research into three categories : (1) survey research, (2) adaptive research, and (3) fundamental research. For the Third World scholars, he recommended the first two types while the third type should be left to the developed nations. As regards the causes he goes on to say that, "it is often costly and to be worth doing it must be very well done, with an aptitude and sensibility which are too rare in the new states" (Shils 1965 : 270).

To my mind, Shils' proposition is an untenable one as all researches are not very costly. In India, we witnessed C.V. Raman winning the Nobel Prize as early as in 1930. In the field of anthropology and social sciences, there is a wide scope and a pressing need for further emphasis on fundamental research. One fears that development-oriented applied research is over-shadowing as the former has no immediate practical value. It is interesting that in his Asian experiences in this context Alatas has pleaded for a similar emphasis for the Third World scholars (Alatas 1976).

A time has come when every community of social sciences (including anthropology) has to determine their own methods, techniques, and models for research. Any adaptation of a foreign model can take place only after a very critical examination of its applicability, suitability and usefulness. While in the West people are moving into a new area of study, i.e., the study of 'overdevelopment', in the developing societies like ours there is an urgent need to conduct more studies in the problems of "backwardness". The problems of urbanisation and industrialisation in several parts of the world present diverse socio-cultural implications and need to be tackled differently. The Colonial past has to be studied and reformulated in a meaningful historical context. Problems of transplantation of the social sciences to the developing societies, reference to which has been made earlier, have to be studied.

There is, again increasing interest in the study of tribes in the historical and archaeological context as the functional-structural approach has failed to bring out the correct appraisal of tribal situations in India.

The study of sacred complexes, temple organisation, occultism and mysticism the complexity of festivals and numerous rituals, the civilizational regions in context with

Indian civilization, etc., are now receiving priorities in India, which incidentally go to emphasise the sphere of fundamental research.

I can only conclude by sharing with you my fond hope that this World Congress will provide a turning point in our common endeavour of rationalising our studies in social sciences, in general; and anthropology, in particular. I am sure, Anthropology for the future, which is being envisaged will keep the aforesaid in mind and will allow the anthropologists of the developing countries to play its due role.

December 10, 1978 L.P. VIDYARTHI

NOTES

1. Refer Vidyarthi : "Current Trends in World Anthropology" and "The Rise of World Anthropology as reflected through the International Congresses (1934-1978)". Some extracts from the first book have been reproduced in the paper presented at Paris in the Round Table Conference organised by the International Social Science Council during its Silver Jubilee Celebration in July 1977.
2. Refer to the Presidential address of the Earl of Onslow in the London Congress in 1934. He says : ". . . I think it was Professor Malinowski who exploded this idea– at any rate as regards the anthropologists of today. He points out in his interesting article on the rationalisation of anthropo logy that anthropologists of a previous generation preferred to study 'man dead rather than alive'. It was 'the science of skulls and skeletons of pleistocene or neolithic man', but the modern anthropologist is of a different temper. . ." (1934, p. 17).
3. Referring to the recognition of such a trend in anthropology a Soviet Ethnographer, Y.V. Averkiyeva, (1974 : 312) observes : "Beginning with the 1950s we observe a feverish search for a 'theory of development'. In fact, even an anthropology of development emerged. By the end of 1950 this search took the form of 'renaissance of evolutionism'. Vividly expressed in connection with the centenary of the publication of Darwin's 'Origin of Species' when, Steward, the well-known anthropologist described it, there was a 'Universal proclamation' of evolutionism. . ."
4. The need for Indianness in Social Science was first emphasised in my paper "History of Social Anthropology in India : A Preliminary Observation" presented in the Sixth International Congress of Anthropological and Ethnological Sciences held at Moscow 1964. It

was further elaborated in several other publications (e.g., Vidyarthi 1966, 1976 and 1978).

5. In order to highlight Gandhi's contribution to Social Sciences, we organised a Seminar on Gandhi and Social Sciences, in the year 1969. The proceedings of which have been published in a book form. The twenty two papers included in this book are divided into four parts : (1) Gandhian Philosophy, (2) Gandhian approach to Social issue, (3) Gandhian approach to economic issues, and (4) Gandhian approach to political issues.
   In order to study in depth Gandhian approach to the tribal problems a doctoral thesis has just been completed and submitted under the supervision of the author by Mrs. Savitri Sinha, Fellow, Khadi and Village Industries Commission.
6. Rabindra Nath Tagore and his disciples wrote profusely on the theme of rural reconstruction and tribal development. Some of these have been published by his institute which he founded. Mention may be made of the unique contribution by Premchand Lal, *Rural Reconstruction in India*, Leonard Elmhirst, *Our Contribution at Sriniketan*, and Sudhir Sen on *Rural Economics*. Kali Mohan Ghosh under the guidance of Tagore himself published two volumes on Village Studies as early as 1925-26. In addition, there are numerous, papers, notes and other writings the bibliography on which have been prepared and published (Bhattacharya 1961).
7. On this theme there are numerous publications by historians, indologists, social philosophers, and a few sociologists. Mention may be made of K.M. Kapadia and M.A. Aiyyangar : The recent paper by the author entitled, "An Anthropological Concept of Development : India A Case Study", presented in the Ninth International Sociological Conference at Uppsala is an analysis of the concept of development from an Indian angle.

SUGGESTED READINGS

Aiyyangar, M.A., *Indian Culture and Religious Thought*. Calcutta : University of Calcutta, 1962.

Alatas, S.H., "The Captive Mind and Creative Development", *International Social Science Journal* 26, 1974, 4.

Alatas, S.H., "The Intellectual Captivity and Developing Societies" presented at 30 International Congress of Human Sciences in Asia and North Africa at Maxico, August 3-8, 1976.

Averkiyeva, Y.V., "Neo-evolutionism, Relativism and Racialism" in I.R. Grigulevich and S.V. Kozlov (eds.) *Races and Peoples Contemporary Ethnic and Racial Problems*. Moscow : Progress Publishers, 1974.

Bhattacharya, B., *Community* : Centenary Number, 1961.

Bose, N.K., *Fifty Years of Science in India : Progress of Anthropology and Archaeology*, Calcutta : Indian Science Congress Association, 1963.

Bose, N.K., *Society and Culture of India*, Bombay : Asia Publishing House, 1967.

Darwin, C., *Origin of Species*, New York : The New American Library of World Literature, Inc. (Mentor Book Edition : 1959), 1859.

Diamond, Stanley, "A Revolutionary Discipline", *Current Anthropology* 5, 1964, 432-437.

The Earl of Onslow, *Proceedings of the First International Congress of Anthropological and Ethnological Sciences held in London* : Institut Royal D'Anthropologie, 1934.

Gandhi, M.K., *Harijan*, 1st August, 1936.

Gandhi, M.K., *Constructive Programme*, Ahmedabad, 1942.

Gore, M.S , *American and Social Science in India*, Bombay.

Harris, Marvin, *The Rise of Anthropological Theory*, London : Routledge and Kegan Paul, 1968.

Kapadia, K.M., *Hindu Kinship*, Bombay : Popular Book Depot, 1947.

Kapadia, K.M., *Marriage and Family in India*, Bombay : Oxford University Press, 1966.

Kroeber, A.L., *Anthropology Today : An Encyclopedic Inventory*, Chicago : The University of Chicago Press, 1953.

Lévi-Strauss, C., "On Problems of Process : Theory in Sol Tax *et al* (eds.) *An Appraisal of Anthropology Today*, Chicago : The University of Chicago Press, 1953.

Loubser, Jan J., "The Need for the Indigenization of the Social Sciences" paper presented at the General Conference of National Councils and Analogous Bodies ISSC (UNESCO) Paris : October 24-26, 1977.

Mead, M., "On Problems of Process : Theory in Sol Tax *et al* (eds.) *An Appraisal of Anthropology Today*, Chicago : The University of Chicago Press, 1953.

Myrdal, Gunnar, *Asian Drama*, Vol. I, London : Penguin Books, 1968.

Nakane, Chie, *Human Relations in Japan*, Tokyo : Ministry of Foreign Affairs, Japan, 1972.

Sarana, G. and D.P. Sinha, "Status of Socio-cultural Anthropology in India". *Annual Review Anthropology*, Vol. 5, UNESCO Paris, 1976.

Shils, Edward, "Scientific Development in the New States" in Ruth Gruber (ed.), *Science and the Nations*, New York : Pyramid Books, 1965.

Sinha, S.C., "Is there an Indian Tradition in Social/Cultural Anthropology : Retrospect and Prospect", *Journal of Indian Anthropological Society*, 6, 1971, 1-14.

Srivastava, R.S., *Sri Aurobindo and the Theories of Evolution*, Varanasi : Choukhamba Sanskrit Series Office, 1968.

Tax, Sol (ed.), *Current Anthropology*, 1.1. 1960.

Tendulkar, D.G., *Mahatma Gandhi*, 4, Bombay, 1954.

Thomas, William L., Jr., and Pikelis, A.M. (eds.) *Current Anthropology : A Supplement to Anthropology Today*, Chicago : The University of Chicago Press, 1956.

Vidyarthi, L.P., "Researches in Social Sciences in India", *Social Science Information*, 5.1. 1966.

Vidyarthi, L.P., *Current Trends in World Anthropology*, Delhi : Concept Publishing Company, 1978a.

Vidyarthi, L.P., *The Rise of World Anthropology as Reflected Through the International Congress (1934-1978)*, Delhi : Concept Publishing Company, 1978b.

Vidyarthi, L.P., *Rise of Anthropology in India : A Social Science Orientation Delhi*, Concept Publishing Company, 1978c.

Vidyarthi, L.P., B.N. Sahay & B.K. Srivastava, *Gandhi and Social Sciences*, New Delhi : Bookhive, 1970.

TWO

Charles Frantz

SCHOLARS OF THE CHAIR
Selected Characteristics of the Presidents of the American Anthropological Association, 1902-1979

INTRODUCTION

THROUGHOUT its history, a substantial proportion of anthropologists have been interested in the organization of human groups. Among the almost endless variety of such groups are voluntary-membership associations, one category of which is based on scholarly, academic, or disciplinary interests and knowledge. Anthropological associations or societies are one variant of this category; but in turn, they vary in terms of whether their membership is international, national, or subnational; and whether membership is formally or informally restricted by gender, language, religious belief or affiliation, level of education, type of employment, or professional experience.

This paper will examine some aspects of the largest anthropological society in the world, the American Anthropological Association. In particular, it will focus on selected data about those who have occupied its highest office, the presidency, from its inception in 1902 through 1979. It is part of a larger study of the Association's formal and informal charters, organization, and dynamic processes which have interested me. The Association—as well as the discipline of anthropology—is being studied in terms of its relationships with other anthropological associations, with non- anthropological societies, councils, foundations, and governments; with educational and research institutions, particularly universities and museums; and with intellectual, social, cultural, economic, and political institutions and movements in the United States, and even internationally.[1]

The main body of my paper will attend to data about 18 selected characteristics of those who have been presidents of the American Anthropological Association (hereafter, the A.A.A.) since 1902. No assumption is made in this paper that any of these characteristics are primary or necessarily determine other characteristics, although an association between two or more characteristics frequently occurs. I do assume, however, following Max Weber and Max Gluckman, that person and office are interrelated, and that both of these are enmeshed in wider social systems. This paper eschews analyzing the actual performance of individuals while occupying the office of president, even though such a study would be of considerable interest. It is thus not an inquiry into leadership, but rather modestly assembles selected data about the persons who were elected to be leaders.

The sources of data used in this study include obituaries, autobiographies, biographies and memoirs, encyclopedias, A.A.A. presidential candidate information sheets, official proceedings of the Association, general historical accounts, and oral interviews and correspondence with presidents and their colleagues and relatives. Almost complete data[2] on 18 characteristics were obtained, and any exceptions are noted in the text. Some slight variations, e.g., in dates, were encountered, but multiple checks for reliability or validity were possible in almost all cases. Data on a number of additional characteristics of presidents are excluded from this paper, either because they were too fragmentary or they have not yet been assembled or analyzed.[3]

The Association and its Presidency

Since it was founded in 1902, the A.A.A. has been the main anthropological society, embracing all subfields or disciplines, in North America. Membership has always been open to individuals of any nationality, although consistently and progressively an overwhelming proportion have been residents of the U.S.A. Initially membership was elective, being based principally upon professional anthropological activities, but later it became non-elective. Various constitutional, administrative, and programmatic changes have been made since 1902, but a number of major changes were introduced in 1947. This sharp break (1947) in continuity will be used to categorize and discuss much of the data about the Association's presidents. The formal governing structure of the A.A.A. has included a President, several Vice-Presidents (from 1947, only one Vice-President, and later a President-Elect), Secretary, Treasurer, Executive Committee (from 1947, an Executive Board), Editor, Program Chairman of the Annual Meeting Council, and various Committees. Almost all these were elective offices, although some became appointive in later years, as was the employment of various officers in 1947 and afterward to execute administrative and programmatic responsibilities.

Any professional and elected member (called "Fellow" for some three decades) was eligible to hold presidential office. From 1902 to 1930, and during 1933 and 1934, each president held office for two years; but in all other years, the tenure of office was for only a single year. In 1947, the year of major reorganization, two persons served as president, each for less than a year. A total of 63 different persons have served as president of the A.A.A. during its seventy-eight years of history.

Selected Characteristics of the Presidents

Data on eighteen characteristics of the 63 presidents will be grouped into four categories: (a) before election, (b) at election, (c) after election, and (d) a combination of these three time periods. The last category involves a single criterion, the year of election into membership of the National Academy of Sciences, which is the major honorary national scientific institution in the U.S.A.

Place of Birth

All but ten of the presidents were born in the United States. They were born in 23 different states, with the largest numbers in Massachusetts (8), New York (7), and Pennsylvania (5). A disproportionate number came from Iowa (4), Nebraska (2), South Dakota (2), and California (1). The remaining ten presidents were born in eight nations outside the U.S.A.

Since reorganization, a significant increase has occurred in the number of presidents born in the western; and secondly,

Midwestern states. Among foreign-born presidents, only three of the total of ten have been elected since reorganization.

Ethnic-Biological Background

All presidents have been of European background except for Hsu (1978, Chinese) and possibly Hough (1923-24, European and American Indian mixture ?).

Age at First Marriage

All but five presidents were married. The mean age when they first took vows was 29.3 years, ranging from Wallace (1972) at 19 to MacCurdy (1931) at 56. The mean age[4] at first marriage slowly declined after 1935, and after World War II all but seven married below the mean.

Level of Education

All but eight presidents were awarded doctoral degrees; three (Nelson, Jenness, Judd) were recipients of masters' degrees, two (Putnam, Holmes) had bachelors' degrees, two (Hodge, Saville) received high school diplomas, and one (McGee), the first president, was self taught. Boas, the third president, (1907-08), was the first who possessed a doctorate, although it was in the discipline of geography. Dixon (1913-14) was the first president to hold a Ph.D. in anthropology. Since 1946, all presidents have held the Ph.D. prior to assuming office, and all but one (Murdock, 1955) were in the field of anthropology.

Institutions which Awarded Doctorates

Of the 55 presidents who received doctoral degrees prior to assuming office, 46 were in anthropology; nine were awarded in the disciplines of geography, psychology, natural history, medicine, geology (or chemistry ?), theology, biology (?) and sociology. Of the 46 Ph. Ds. in anthropology, two were received in England. The remaining 44 were obtained from a strikingly limited number of universities in the U.S.A. : Harvard (14), Columbia (13), Chicago (9), Yale (2), Pennsylvania (2), and the University of California at Berkeley (4). All but the last of these universities are privately owned. The first president to have received a doctorate in anthropology from a governmentally-owned institution was Beals, in 1951. Of the six female presidents of the Association, five received their Ph.D.s from Columbia University, and the other from the University of California at Berkeley.

Some significant changes with respect to which universities provided doctoral education in anthropology to future presidents before and after the reorganization are apparent. In the pre-reorganization period, all twenty presidents received their doctorates from non-governmental institutions. Since 1947, four of the 31 presidents have received their doctorates from one public university, the University of California at Berkeley. In the private sector, the greatest increase in spawning A.A.A. presidents has been shown by the University of Chicago; eight post-reorganization presidents, in contrast to one during the prereorganization period, received their Ph. Ds. from that institution.

Age at Receiving Doctorate

The mean age at which presidents obtained their doctoral degrees was 28.8 years, and the figures for males and females are virtually identical. The range was from 21 (Cooper) and 23 (Boas, Hrdlicka) to 42 (MacCurdy). The three youngest presidents received doctorates in disciplines other than anthropology, however, as did Parsons in sociology at the age of 24. Shapiro, also at age 24, was the youngest president to have been awarded a Ph.D. in anthropology. Almost identical mean ages of receiving doctorates before and after the Association's reorganization were realized: 29 and 28.7 years, respectively.

Vice-Presidential Experience

Before the 1947 reorganization, several persons annually were elected Vice-Presidents. From 1947 through 1951, however, only one individual was elected Vice-President; and serving in that office did not automatically result in accession to the presidency. Between 1902 and 1951, there were 55 different persons who were Vice-Presidents. Of this number, exactly half were subsequently elected to the presidency. One of them (MacCurdy) served as Vice-President for eleven years. Of the remaining number who were not elected to the presidency, one (Dorsey) served as Vice-President for ten years. Constitutional changes in 1952 replaced the office of Vice-President with that of President-Elect, and provided that the President-Elect automatically became the President in the following year.

Thus far, we have examined seven characteristics of presidents prior to their assuming office. Now we turn to describe eight further characteristics of these men and women at the time of their election to the presidency.

Age

The mean age at election to the office of president has been 55, ranging from 38 (Dixon, in 1913) to 69 (Hsu, in 1978). The mean age was significantly lower during two periods, i.e., in 1913-19 (three of the four presidents) and immediately after reorganization, in 1947-54 (seven of the eight presidents). Since 1954, the mean age of presidents has increased gradually.

Sex

Six of the Association's 63 presidents have been females. Parsons was the first to be elected, in 1941, followed by five others from 1946 onward. (In the history of the A.A.A., there have been only seven women among the 80 Vice-Presidents and Presidents-Elect. Fletcher was the earliest, serving from 1904 to 1911, and she also was the only female Vice-President not elected later to become President. Also during the Association's history, three of the nineteen Secretaries and three of nineteen Treasurers have been women).

Marital Status

When elected to office, 54 presidents were married, three were widowed, one was divorced, four were unmarried, and the status of one (Spier) has not been ascertained. There was no change in these proportions before and after the A.A.A.s' reorganization. The incumbent president (Bohannan) is the only anthropologist to be in a divorced status when elected to office.

Number of Children

At the time of their election, 57 presidents who were married had a mean of 1.93 children. Twelve of this number, however, had no children, whereas two (Boas, Parsons) tied in having the largest families, six offspring each. The mean number of children in presidential families was slightly greater in the 1938-42 period (Sapir, Jenness, Parsons, Kidder), but otherwise there has been little variation over the decades.

Place of Residence

Except for Jenness (1939), living in Canada, all presidents were residents of the U.S.A. when elected. However, considerable change occurred in the residential location of presidents prior to and following reorganization in 1947. The distribution of presidents in the two periods was as follows: Northeastern states, 13 and 16 ; Midwestern states, 2 and 7 ; Western states, 3 and 8 ; and Southern states and the District of Columbia, 10 and 2. The greatest shift was in the last region, and reflects the increased national dispersion of anthropologists : All ten presidents in the former period were located in Washington, D.C., whereas the later two resided in North Carolina and Texas.

Subfields or Disciplines

Occasionally it has been difficult to assign one principal subfield to A.A.A. presidents, as they have made contributions to different branches of anthropology. Using the best available information, however, it seems that 41 presidents were basically ethnologists or social-cultural anthropologists, 16 were archaeologists, 4 were physical or biological anthropologists, and 2 were linguistic anthropologists. All six female presidents belong to the first category. Since reorganization, the percentage of presidents whose speciality was archaeology declined somewhat, while that of ethnologists and physical anthropologists increased. However, for the last eleven years, all the presidents have been specialists in social-cultural anthropology.

Type of Employer

One president (Parsons, in 1941) was not employed at the time of being elected. Of the remaining, 46 were attached to twenty-one different universities ; 30 were at eleven privately-owned and 16 were at ten governmentally-owned ones. The remaining 16 presidents were employed by museums or research institutions ; six of these were in privately-owned and ten were in governmentally-owned ones (especially the U.S. National

Museum and the Bureau of American Ethnology). Significant changes occurred after the 1947 reorganization as to the employers for whom A.A.A. presidents were working at the time of their election. The number employed in private universities during the two periods rose from 12 to 18, but in public universities a more striking increase occurred, from three to 18. The number of presidents who worked in governmental museums or other agencies dropped dramatically from nine to zero, and the number who were attached to private museums and research organizations fell from five to two. Mead, in 1960, was the last president to be associated primarily with a museum.

Rank or Title

The 46 presidents who were affiliated with universities at the time of their election held the following academic ranks : Full Professor, 42 ; Associate Professor, one (Kroeber) ; Assistant Professor, two (Dixon, Benedict) ; and Lecturer, one (MacCurdy). Since reorganization, however, all 31 presidents who were university teachers held the rank of Full Professor.

A few other data about presidents of the Association have been tabulated, and are presented now.

Age at Death

Thirty-seven of the 63 presidents had died prior to 1979. Their mean age at death was 72.9, ranging from 48 (Bennett) to 91 (Hodge). Almost no difference occurs in the mean age of those who died before and after reorganization in 1947. None of those who held the presidency before reorganization are still living.

Age of Living Presidents

Twenty-six of the A.A-A.s' presidents are still alive. Their mean age is 68, and the range is from 54 (Adams) to 81 (Murdock).

Age of Election into the National Academy of Sciences

Unlike the previous seventeen criteria, election into the United States' most prestigious honorary scientific society is less than universal. Furthermore, such election into the National

Academy of Sciences may have occurred prior to, during, or after the year/s in which they were the chief officers of the A.A.A. Of the 63 presidents of the Association, only 30 have been elected into the Academy at any time. In ten cases, election into the Academy has preceded presidency of the Association, and in two cases both elections happened in the same years. The mean age of A.A.A. presidents when they were elected into the Academy is 56.1, or about one year more than the mean age of being elected president of the Association. Of the 30 presidents who were elected into the Academy, all but two (Mead and deLaguna, in 1975) were men ; in both women's cases, election into the Academy followed incumbency as president of the A.A.A. Finally, a significant trend may be noted by comparing the pre- and post-reorganization periods : Only four of the thirteen presidents elected to the Academy before 1947 held the presidential office prior to entering the Academy ; in contrast, since 1947, thirteen of the fifteen presidents held this office before their election into the Academy.

Discussion

During the 78-year history of the Association, a number of noticeable changes took place with respect to eighteen characteristics of its presidents. However, it may be noted firstly that almost no change occurred before and after reorganization in 1947 with respect to four characteristics, i.e., age at which doctorate was received, marital status, number of offspring, and age at death.

On the other hand, the level of education attained by presidents has increased, and substantively it has solely been undertaken, at the doctoral level, in anthropology. Increasingly, presidents have been specialists in social-cultural anthropology ; they are full-time faculty members, holding the rank of Full Professor ; and proportionately more are in governmentally— rather than privately-owned universities. Paralleling this has been a slowly rising mean age at which individuals are elected president. Also related to this is the datum that an increasing proportion of presidents do not get elected into the National Academy of Sciences until after they have held the A.A.A. office. Furthermore, it is clear that in recent decades the number of female presidents has risen. In addition, the Western and Midwestern states have become increasingly important, not only as the birthplace of future presidents, but also as the locale where they received their Ph. D.s and where they held university positions at the time of their election.

In contrast, the proportion of archaeologists elected into the presidency has declined considerably since 1947, and even more so have anthropologists holding appointments with governmental museums or agencies. Finally, it may be noted that the mean age at which Association presidents first marry has declined over the decades.

Most of these data about the changing characteristics of A.A.A. presidents seem to reflect general changes in U.S. anthropology during the twentieth century, i.e., the increasing importance of universities rather than museums as centres of prestige and/or research ; of public over private universities ; of Midwestern, Western, and Southern in comparison to Northeastern universities ; the rise of female enrollment in graduate studies ; the rise in the general level of education in the discipline of anthropology; and the growth of specialization within and between academic disciplines.[5] Furthermore, all but the first of these changes are similar to general demographic changes in the whole of the nation. Finally, it may be noted that A.A.A. presidents have been dissimilar to the general population with respect to three characteristics : marital status, number of offspring, and ethnic-biological background.

Concluding Remarks

This study of selected characteristics of the presidents of the American Anthropological Association between 1902 and 1979 has indicated some of the ways in which they have been similar to, or different from, other members of the A.A.A. and the U.S. public at large. Since it is only a case study, generalizations are not possible about anthropological (or other scholarly) societies in general, whether or not they are located in the U.S.A. Perhaps this study can stimulate further research into such matters, as well as to undertaking inquiries into the linkages between individual anthropologists (presidents and otherwise), the discipline/s of anthropology, and the changing intellectual, social, economic, and political milieux of the

United States and the wider world. A study of the actual performance of presidents, in relation to other officers, members, and the public, would be especially valuable. A better understanding of the A.A.A. and other organizations may be achieved when data become available about decisions, choices, and actions made by officers, committee members, and others. Associational or organizational life can best be analyzed by combining formal and informal, as well as static/structural and dynamic, data and points of view.

NOTES

1. I have presented some relevant data in two previous papers delivered at Annual Meetings of the American A nthropological Association, dealing with the organizational history of the A.A.A. add its relationships with universities, museums, and selected areas of life in the U.S.A. Material in those papers, as well as the present one, are to be incorporated into a future book.
2. Some data for 1903 and 1904, when W.J. McGee was president, have not been located, principally because the Official Proceedings of the A.A.A.'s Annual Meetings do not seem to have been published. With respect to a few presidents, letters of inquiry were not answered.
3. Such data include the presidents' dates of divorce, number of children, ethnic background or identity, number of siblings, birth order in their natal families, pre-university education and experiences that might have stimulated their interest in anthropology, years of teaching and research experience, horizontal (lateral) and vertical job mobility, and so forth.
4. The data on President Spier are uncertain.
5. The supporting data for this summary statement are found in the two papers referred to in Note 1, as well as in publications of Stocking, Darnell, and several other recent writers.

THREE

David G. Mandelbaum

ANTHROPOLOGY AND THE CHALLENGES OF DEVELOPMENT

THE GENERAL topic for these plenary sessions, "Anthropology and the Challenges of Development" poses a central question. What can anthropologists contribute in aid of development efforts? The surge of development programs during the past three decades has been led by economists, economic planners, economic administrators. Technologists implemented the plans that were cast in the mould of economists' thought. Relatively little consideration was given to studies by anthropologists or other social scientists. At the beginning, the economists' monopoly seemed appropriate because the basic goal was the alleviation of poverty. Hundreds of millions of the world's people lived and still live in dire poverty, do not have sufficient food or adequate shelter, clothing, health resources, educational opportunities to be able to lift themselves above a level of bare subsistence and sometimes of near starvation.

Some very substantial increases in productivity have resulted from these Post-World War II programs. Yet many in the newly developing countries still suffer from the squeeze of widespread, acute poverty. One common condition is that the poorest groups in these societies have not benefited much, if any, from the increases in material production. Other difficulties have arisen in social dislocations, cultural discord, and environmental damage that have sometimes come along with gains in material output. Too often such gains have added little to a people's sense of well-being and life improvement. These shortcomings result from many causes, but one frequent element lies in how development plans have usually been formulated and executed—from the top down or imposed by central authorities on villagers. At the beginning of the push for development, it could scarcely have been otherwise, given the resources required for planning, the political conditions of the times, and the separation in understanding, even within a country, between the planners and those for whom the plans were made.

After some thirty years of partial successes and some utter failures, the inherent defects of narrowly economic planning have become evident. Effective, enduring development requires much more than increases in Gross National Product (GNP). To achieve sustained development in a country, its people have to benefit and also to feel that they have benefited. Its leaders and people have to establish appropriate roles and equable relations that are personally rewarding and socially accepted. They have to rework the system of their society and culture to cope with the new conditions, reconciling disparate sectors, establishing revised channels for conflict expression and conflict resolution, making relevant knowledge available to all social strata, linking their society with world society (cf. Dalton 1971; Epstein 1972, 1977; Penny 1972; Pitt 1976; Schneider 1975). At the same time, they have to try to mitigate the larger obstacles to development, particularly that of excessive growth of population.

This building, meshing, and mitigating cannot be accomplished in a single leap or over one generation or by exclusive concentration on economic factors. If the improvements that have so far been achieved are to be expanded, development plans too have to be expanded. Legislation has been a common means by which planners have tried to enhance economic aims, as through land reform laws intended to promote greater social as well as economic equality. Laws can indeed be powerful instruments for development, but only if they command wide public support, are guarded by administrative officials, and are bolstered by adequate resources for enforcement. In more than a few instances, however, well-meaning legislation has been ineffectual or even counterproductive. Some laws have been enacted more as ritual gestures toward a development goal devoutly to be desired for some indefinite future than as a standard devotedly to be upheld in the immediate present.

All plans for development have greater chances for success if the relevants cultural and social factors are integrated into the planning. That integration, however, should not add yet another extraneous load on already overburdened planners. Social and cultural considerations must be so presented that they are plainly appropriate to the problems at hand and are clearly useful for makers of development decisions. There is no gain from deluging planners with data they cannot deploy, with recommendations too wordy to be carefully read or too abstruse to be readily understood. There is, however, great potential gain in broadening development policies so that they include significant forces that have hitherto been largely overlooked.

All the social and behavioural sciences can be tapped for this purpose. Anthropologists have special resources to offer (Mandelbaum 1978). Their emphasis on a holistic view disposes them to take into account the social matrix in which particular problems are embedded. Their practice of field work directs attention to development as perceived from within, how the people understand, accept, or reject introduced innovations (cf. Srinivas 1977 : 3 ; Wallman 1977). Anthropologists are also inclined to relate what they learn in the microview to the macroview, to some general perspective on the human career (cf. Patch and McMorrow 1977 : 683-684). Comparative studies done by anthropologists have often taken a wide range, sometimes a global span. Such scope of analysis is well suited for the study of the global forces that increasingly affect the peoples of the modern world. No group is isolated from these forces. All must cope with them whether they do so blindly, in ignorance of possible options, or with some informed, considered procedure.

Seen in the longest human perspective, development is part of a series of cultural thresholds crossed by humankind. At each successive crossing people gain greater control over their environment and enrich their material circumstances, as they did when some learned to produce their food through agriculture and herding rather than to depend only on hunting and gathering. Soon after came the great social invention of civilization with its characteristic components of specialization of work, cities, state organization, writing. Very recently, as human history runs, some groups learned how to command vast amounts of energy through mechanical and industrial means. And just a few generations later there came the upsurge in science together with the highly effective, cumulative applications of science. In making a transition, a people share certain similar consequences with others who have done so, but different groups have crossed these cultural thresholds at different times, in quite different ways, impelled by differing reasons (cf. Eisenstadt 1977 : 62-64).

From the vantage of this long view, current development efforts make up a movement to enable all peoples to benefit from the newly opened cultural potentials. But it is not enough to take over more efficient tools and agricultural procedures or to import tourists and export labour. That may result in some quick economic growth but does not necessarily lead to lasting development, to being able to maintain a continuous flow of the material benefits, to achieving social and personal rewards made possible by new technology. If a people are to maintain higher productivity, they must also establish an appropriate social and cultural infra-structure for such development (cf. Uphoff and Ilchman 1972 : 86-92; Belshaw 1972). That infra-structure includes adapted, revised institutions, associations, education, roles, rewards, values. Social capital has to be built no less than physical capital. As the experiences after World War II demonstrated, a nation's material capital may be devastated but if the survivors are able to draw on their social capital, the material destruction can quickly be overcome.

In the building of an adapted social infra-structure, political leaders do not have to try to jettison all the traditional ways forthwith. Quite to the contrary, they are often best advantaged if they keep those elements of their traditional culture that are compatible with development and base their innovative programs on them. Some traditional patterns neither hinder nor advance the work of development. Other traditional institutions that do seem inimical have been, in various instances, reinterpreted without being abandoned, reshaped without losing their identification, or gradually phased out. Some patterns have indeed been abruptly terminated and sometimes justifiably so. Occasionally that termination has been massive, achieved through revolutionary armed conflict. While such upheavals may be justified at certain junctures of some societies, successful activists must still cope with the problems of achieving development after they have won the struggle. In meeting these problems they too have to build an adapted social-cultural infra-structure.

Whether the shift from the previous culture is gradual or sharp, each traditional culture is amenable to different modes of being adapted. There is no monolithic culture type that can be labelled "traditional", whose ways are always and totally opposed to modern developments. But the processes of establishing rooted development usually take considerable time, often involve internal conflicts, and are best conducted according to some sequence of appropriate changes, social and cultural as well as economic. One broad task for social anthropologists is to study the possible sequences of social-cultural change open for a particular people at a particular time and to make recommendations for policy and action. Such recommendations are best presented as a set of alternative options with an assessment of the probable outcomes of following one policy alternative or another.

Development studies by anthropologists have dealt, for the most part, with much narrower and more specific matters than the grander issues of national policy alternatives. The local tasks are not to be spurned; they can be useful not only in a restricted arena, but can also provide data and ideas for general policy formulations. Whatever the scope, a study is enhanced if it can be based on an overall frame of ideas about development that has been considered, discussed, and debated by anthropologist among others. That frame of concepts should include the general requirements common to many developing countries and also allow for the special circumstances of particular countries, of broad areas, or of internal regions.

One of the common general requirements is that of welding a more closely articulated social-political entity than existed before. Another is the establishment of governmental bureaucracies competent to fulfil the expanded services that are now expected of government. There is also the question of how best to relate a developing society with the international environment in which its people must now operate. Still another common dilemma is how to fashion institutions that have built into them an openness to continual adaptation while retaining established symbols that provide comforting assurance of continuity.

There is no one road to development and certainly not the identical sequence traversed by countries now deemed to be developed. Whatever course is urged or coerced by planners and political leaders, each major group within a nation eventually judges what the purpose of development is for them and for whom the development bells toll. The outcome of any model of development depends ultimately on the effectiveness of their participation (cf. De Kadt 1974 : 3-14; Eisenstadt 1977 : 64-68). That is to say, the people of each country judge what quality of life they aspire to, and the qualify of life, it is becoming realized, is not to be measured solely or even primarily by the index of a nation's overall GNP.

It is true that before other measures for development can be effective certain basic conditions must prevail. A people cannot do much construction for the future if many of them are struggling for mere subsistence survival. Nor can development programs take shape if a state is torn with turmoil, its land more the scene of battles than of building. But given such basic requirements, people do respond effectively to programs for development if the programs are presented in terms they can understand and accept. Villagers do not, as has sometimes been alleged, act irrationally in respect to prices and maximization of production, except in the eyes of those who do not understand their usually rational assessment of risk and the consequences of failure. Nor have indigenous entrepreneurs been lacking in most developing societies. What has been lacking is an economic and social environment that will encourage such entrepreneurs. There have been notable improvements in some new nations in recent decades and spectacular advances in certain enclaves, as Professor Foster reports for a village in Mexico and Professor von Furer-Haimendorf for a tribal group in India.

We are accustomed to thinking of development as process of catching-up by the poorer countries, in the course of which they may receive some assistance from the more affluent countries. But even among the more affluent nations, there is a strongly felt need for internal development. Their people too are trying to adapt their ways and their resources to overcome dangerous dilemmas and debilitating problems. For example, an anthropological study entitled "Energy and the Quality of Life" indicates that per capita energy use and quality of life are related in complex ways. The study indicates that increased availability and use of electrical and other energy sources does not always improve the quality of life (Nader and Beckerman 1978). It is for such reasons that many citizens of the United States have recently expressed, through their votes, their disillusionment with some of the programs for their own development. These programs have fallen short not so much because of lack of funds but rather because of neglect of social and cultural considerations, of continuous evaluation, of widely debated alternate proposals.

When the people of a country become assured that their basic material needs are reasonably well available, then their aspirations for development are likely to turn to the quality of their lives. This concept includes a great many components that are not always mutually compatible or strictly logical. But a leading element is their shared idea that they are entitled to feel self-reliant, autonomous, worthy (or superior) as a people (cf. Wallman 1977 : 11, 14). For that reason even small, impoverished new nations have frequently invested in a costly set of modern appurtenances, from an international airline to a voracious steel mill. Such a symbolic array of technology is supposed to give the nation's people (or at least the ruling group) a sense that they too are worthy of being full participants in the modern world. Paradoxically, the more proficient they became in advanced technology, the more dependent they are on exports and imports, on international monetary and stock markets, on foreign experts and jobs abroad for their own workers (World Bank 1978 : 65-68). So in sustaining continuous development, each people has to nurture their subjective feelings of self-reliance and autonomy while objectively entering into multiple relations of enduring dependence.

There is a growing number of people in many nations,

both in the more and in the less affluent, who realize that a satisfactory quality of life does not necessarily depend on over-increasing economic growth. Development, it is true, must first of all establish reliable provisions of the basic necessities for a physically secured life. But development processes do not stop there. Political leaders and planners have to go on to propose continuous adaptations toward what their people will consider a good life. Gandhi understood this well. Indeed, Professor Srinivas writes that "the approach which Gandhi hacked out for himself through years of struggle is somewhat similar to the method of participant observation practised by the anthropologist. Both aim at understanding people and not merely gathering facts about them" (1977 : 13). The core of Gandhi's teachings on the quality of life may yet be taken to heart more widely through the world.

Anthropologists now have more opportunity than before to contribute to development. Their own ethical and procedural problems in the field have been sufficiently aired to permit such work to proceed apace. Planners and administrators are coming to realize that their previous models have slighted some critical elements, namely the cultures and societies of the people whom and on whom development plans were enacted (cf. World Bank 1978 : 33-42). Anthropologists not only come at development problems from the perspective of the people, they also tend to try to understand particular projects as parts of a larger system. And very frequently, it is the system of social relations and cultural understandings that is critical for the success or failure of projects. For, as we now recognize, development is not only the adaptation of advanced technology and economic programming, nor is it just another term for change. Development consists of purposive efforts by a people, led by public figures and planners, to organize themselves in new technical, cultural, and social ways. These are ways that will enable them to achieve the style and quality of life to which they aspire. When their aspirations shift, the direction of development efforts must shift accordingly.

The Swedish economist, Gunnar Myrdal, is quoted as saying that "... we economists, who monopolize national planning for development, are on the verge of coming to see the necessity of a much broader approach to this planning, (while) our colleagues in the other social sciences, and in the first place, the anthropologists, are not providing us with the information we need" (Nag 1978 : 359). From the accelerated flow of relevant anthropological studies in recent years, it appears that a good many anthropologists are rising to meet this challenge of development.

SUGGESTED READINGS

Belshaw, C.S., "Development : The Contribution of Anthropology", *International Social Science Journal*, 24, 1972, 80-94.

Dalton, George, "Modernizing Village Economies McCaleb Module 3", *Reading*, Mass : Addison-Wesley, 1971.

De Kadt, Emanuel, "Introduction : In Society and Development", E. De Kadt and G. Williams editors, London : Tavistock, 1974, pp. 1-19.

Eisenstadt, Shmuel N., "Sociological Theory and an Analysis of the Dynamics of Civilizations and of Revolutions". In Daedalus, Discoveries and Interpretations, 1977, pp. 59-78.

Epstein, T. Scarlett, "The Dimensions of Rural Development. In Opportunity and Response : Case Studies in Economic Development", T.S. Epstein and H. Penny editors, London : Hurst, 1972, pp. 241-51.

Epstein, T. Scarlett, "The Role of Social Anthropology in Development Studies", In Anthropology in the Development Process, H.M. Mathur editor, New Delhi : Vikas, 1977, pp. 88-103.

Mandelbaum, David G., "The Potentials of Anthropology. In Anthropology for the Future, D.G. Shimkin, S. Tax, and J.W. Morrison eds. Department of Anthropology, University of Illinois, Urbana. *Research Report* 4, 1978, pp. 24-41.

Nader, Laura and Stephen Beckerman, "Energy as it Relates to the Quality and Style of Life, *In Annual Review of Energy* 3, 1978, Palo Alto : Annual Review Inc., 1-28.

Nag, Moni ["M.N."], "Review of Anthropology in the Development Process", H.M. Mathur editor. *In Population and Development Review* 4, 1978, 358-359.

Patch, Richard and Leon McMorrow, "The Anthropology of Development," *American Behavioural Scientist* 20, 1977, 681-692.

Penny, David H., "Development Studies : Some Reflections." In Opportunity and Response : Case Studies in Economic Development, T.S. Epstein and D.H. Penny editors, London : Hurst. 1972, pp. 1-10.

Pitt, David C., "Development from Below." In Development from Below, Anthropologists and Development Situations, D.C. Pitt editor, The Hague : Mouton and Chicago : Aldine, 1976, pp. 7-20.

Schneider, Harold K., "Economic Development and Anthropology. In

Annual Review of Anthropology, B.J. Siegel et al. editors, Palo Alto : *Annual Reviews Inc*. 1975, pp. 271 292.

Srinivas, M.N. "The Dual Cultures of Independent India. Gandhi Memorial Lecture." Banglore : Raman Research Institute, 1977.

Uphoff, Norman T. and Warren F. Ilchman, "The Political Economy of Development." Berkeley : University of California Press, 1972.

Wallman, Sandra, "Introduction. In Perceptions of Development", S. Wallman editor, New York : Cambridge University Press, 1977, pp. 1-17.

World Bank, "World Development Report. Washington, D.C. : The World Bank, 1978.

FOUR

S.R. Charsley

THE SOCIAL ANTHROPOLOGY OF DEVELOPMENT
An Alternative Perspective

THERE are two logically distinct kinds of relationship between social anthropology and development. In this essay I seek to persuade the reader that the less noticed of these has important advantages over the commoner. I note the disadvantages of this latter and attempt to demonstrate that the former is not only theoretically desirable but is also practicable and likely to be useful. This somewhat polemical form of argument should not be taken to imply a hostility towards the more usual kind of development anthropology or any wish to exaggerate differences or to erect barriers between them. My object is only to encourage the more general adoption of a neglected perspective, and one which has the added merit, for this writer, of providing an alternative to the increasingly influential Marxist perspectives on development generally.

Despite all variations and differences of emphasis, Marxists have a strong hand to play in approaching development, is for three basic reasons. They have available to them in the first place a grand conception of world history as a single process and an overall direction of movement : social evolution, class struggle and the centrality of Capitalism both in the contemporary world and on the path to the future, just and inevitable. Though this does not clearly prescribe the change which is progressive in every situation, it does in general mean that there is no fundamental problem about defining development. It is defined by history, understood "scientifically". They have a strong hand secondly because they can offer an account of what is "behind" the relatively obvious, or perhaps purposely confusing, surface of things. They have therefore the basis for saying new things about old situations and for comprehending apparent diversity in terms of high generality. To study development is to study what comes in the way of the perception of exploitative class relationships, what holds back the class struggle and retards the revolution. And to reveal these is not just an intellectual matter. It is the thought-action, the praxis, that creates reality. Thirdly, on top of this commitment to apparently relevant "action", there is the passionate morality which permeates the Marxist perspective and shines through such of its key concepts as "exploitation". This last must surely have considerable appeal for us as anthropologists. As we commute between social universes so strikingly ill-balanced in the material rasources available within them we can scarcely help from time to time reflecting that we obtain a rich man's living from our intimate involvement with the poor. Less parochially, it is clearly a kind of moral and political commitment which answers fairly widely to the need not to stand by, merely observing and profiting in a world of gross inequities. Whether the "action" it offers is more in the nature of science, magic or religion must, however, remain a matter for individual judgement.

The Marxist has therefore distinct advantages, granted only that basic theory be true. One might even wish that it were. But if it is erroneous, as I, aligning myself with Firth (1975; cf. Sachs 1972 : 41) on this issue, believe it to be—and there can be no point in seeking to do more than state this as an axiom for what follows—then it can scarcely provide a suitable perspective for the anthropological study of development. There are of course anthropologists concerned with development who are Marxists, but Marxism's drawback is that it tends to devalue knowledge of the particular kind that anthropologists seek, i.e. of the actions of people within particular and distinctive social and cultural settings. As Barnett (1977 : 24) has it, there arises a problem over "the dialectic of conscience with observation": "there is always an uncomfortable dialogue between the researcher's beliefs and aspirations about and for the world, and what his research shows him the world is like" (see also Copans and Seddon 1978). Certainly, if all explanatory and causal weight is put on larger-scale relationships of dependence (cf. Foster-Carter 1974) and/or on stressing what-is-to-be as the only reality, the relevance of most of what non-Marxist anthropologists know to be important is drained away. The Marxist may well feel that social anthropology, with its empiricist preoccupation with the observation of to him insignificant minutiae, has hitherto been unhelpful for development, has even been an instrument of bourgeois mystification opposed to true development. Terray's ambition to absorb the field of social anthropology into historical materialism as "a particular section "devoted to socio-economic formations in which the capitalist mode of production is absent" (1972 : 184) is well known and leaves little scope for our subject in the field of development.

There is however no need to make the rejection reciprocal. Marxism must be of interest even to "sceptical anthropologists". It has contributed and will no doubt continue to contribute interests and lines of analysis to their thinking, as well as stimulation to a clearer perception of its nature and assumptions. Besides this, Marxism is in many of its manifestations a prime object of study. Its importance and even practical relevance for those who accept it, or may be persuaded to do so, are so great as to put it surely amongst the most crucial belief systems of our time for empirical investigation.

Foster-Carter (1974 : 69) has claimed, with some justification, that "Marxism is the prototype of development theory as such" : "The idea of "development" in social science, meaning the progressive alteration and succession of different socio-economic formations over time, is firmly Marxian in origin". Be that as it may, Marxism certainly provides a basis for the commonest type of relationship between any academic discipline and development. This is the type of approach which takes the nature and positive value of development as given and casts the discipline, anthropology here, in the role of assistant to its furtherance.

There are various senses in which development may be regarded as given and the robustness of the concept undoubtedly arises partly from its ambiguities. It may on the one hand have no more than a formula definition equivalent roughly to "improvement", but without specifying in any way what constitutes such improvement. Apthorpe (1973) treats development in this way, contrasting it with "modernization", the latter being sometimes "nothing other than readings of what in the history or traditions of one society or situation were somehow to be recommended for another" (13). On a formal definition of this kind it is almost impossible to question the desirability of development, though one may question whether something is the best possible development or indeed is actually development at all. Such a notion seems also to underlie other more complex usages and to give an apparent though illusory strength to them. Accompanying it one may find agnostic suppositions—if development involves, then . . ."; or meanings for "development" may be postulated and "indicators" chosen, often largely for their accessibility and convenience; or more positive ideas assuming or asserting that development is an aspect of reality may be found. This last may be no more than a common-sense feeling that there has obviously been a process of development at work in the world and perhaps that its benefits should be spread. It may on the other hand be grounded in elaborated theory such as the Marxist or contemporary American revivals of ecological evolutionism (Poggie and Lynch 1974).

It is in the middle ground that the problem of specifying the ingredients of development is greatest. Belshaw (1972 : 83) for instance, asserts that " 'Development' represents an increase in the capacities of a society to organize for its own objectives, and to carry out its programmes more effectively", and finds it necessary to distinguish this from "growth" and "performance", the latter being whether "the people in the society in question" like it. He is undoubtedly pointing to important differences, but are they his discoveries or his inventions? The sceptic might suggest that the standard in these matters is set by the self-image of those who are both powerful in the world and sufficiently self-confident to feel no need to attend to any reference group beyond themselves. The nature of development may have seemed relatively clear, for instance, when a self-confident U.S.A. exported Community

Development to India in the 1950s (Dube 1958). As late as 1969 indeed, George Foster was writing : "About the broad objectives of most technical aid programmes, there is little question", though "In other periods (e.g. the British colonial) a major conflict has existed" (176/7). At the same time no less a person than George Dalton (1971), stressing the economist's view of development "as a long-run, continuing process of new, improved, and diversified activities and technology, so that community income rises continually" (275), was yet able to write "We in industrialized, modernized, developed America . . ." (279). But he was going on to refer to "our national strife" and the rot had already set in. Self-doubt, questioning and looking elsewhere for models were manifestly more prominent in that quarter as the 1970s proceeded (Mead 1974; Adams 1974).

If arbitrariness lurks around development in general, specifically economic development may seem clearer. Surely, it may be felt, wealth must always be central and to have greater wealth must always be more developed than to have less. Or must it ? Orthodox thinking among development economists has changed radically from the 1950s (Oshima 1977), with an apparent increase in responsiveness to the problems of "lesser developed countries" as they have been actually observed in recent years. Equity has appeared as a leading consideration and even such noble, if somewhat open, aspirations as providing for "the realization of the potential of human personality" or "the true fulfilment of human potential" replace mere growth in national income as 'true' development (Seers 1972). We even have firmly before us the possibility that our own types of wealthy, urban, industrial society represent "an historical culde-sac" (Foster-Carter 1974 : 93), that if economic development be continued growth, then that development is a recipe for disaster (Meadows 1972).

The alternative—and there is only one in so far as it is a straight negation—is not to take development as given, nor to enlist anthropology amongst its acolytes. It is to treat development as a sphere of human activity, including the somewhat rarefied definitional activity of scholars, which anthropology may investigate as it is well used to investigating other spheres of activity, designated economic, political, religious, etc. Bastide has argued somewhat similarly in putting forward his proposal for an applied anthropology as "a theoretical science of practice" : it is not to be "oriented toward action and planning; it analyses that action and that planning as the old anthropology analysed kinship systems, economic and political institutions, spontaneous processes of change, and with exactly the same techniques of approach" (1973 : 180/1).[1] There is no necessity, that is to say, to see development as an "applied" interest for anthropology. It is as legitimate and desirable, or as I shall argue more so, to regard it as a new specialism generated by the changing world in which anthropologists operate, within the central body of "pure" anthropology.

This is not of course to say anything in substance new. There has always in British social anthropology been a strong tendency for the anthropologist to distance himself from the projects of those in authority and to "apply" the subject, not in the more active American fashion (Foster 1969), but by the evaluation of implications and the study of unforeseen consequences (Mair 1956). My object is therefore merely to consolidate a distinction within the types of work which already exist. For this purpose it may be useful to specialize terms already in use. Anthropology is not in the habit of giving meaning to the syntactical form of the names of its specialisms but it may nevertheless be convenient to do so here. By analogy with the kind of distinction expressed in our sister discipline by names such as "religious sociology" and "the sociology of religion", the former referring to sociology in the service of religion, the latter to the open-minded sociological study of religion, I suggest that the first alternative be termed "development anthropology", the second "the anthropology of development". This is not to erect any barrier against the mutual relevance of studies made under one banner or the other but merely to draw attention to a distinctness of perspectives.

But what exactly is it that this anthropology of development is to study? From a consideration of the other specialized areas of the subject it must be clear that no tight and undisputed definition is required for a practically useful field to be distinguished. While even a residual holism holds sway, as perhaps it is bound to as long as studies are empirically based in first-hand experience of living contexts, definitions of this kind are not of the greatest consequence. But in fact it is probably not difficult to produce an adequate formal definition of the anthropology of development. One may say that it is concerned with those social fields in which people seek to secure improvements in their own or in other people's performance, either in tasks they are already performing or through new tasks which they may take up. It is the actors, and this is crucial part of the difference in perspective which I am trying to establish, who determine what constitutes "improvement" and how it is to be sought. No-one's determination is ever final, and dispute, misunderstanding and conflict are likely to be common features of the social fields set up by efforts to alter patterns of behaviours. This is particularly so where the social and cultural distance between initiators and subjects is great, as it often is in the fields most likely to interest anthropologists. Such fields are not of course to be found everywhere and all the time but they are increasingly generated across the world by the *dirigiste* temper of our age. Despite this they represent only a small part of the total pattern of social change. It has yet to be demonstrated indeed, that they even represent a significant part, however great their salience may be for at least some of those involved.

The focus therefore is development activity, viewed as consisting in the seeking of improvements. The anthropologist is, however, inevitably concerned not only with the search itself but also with the various social contexts within which it takes place, the structures, institutions and processes which form its environments. He will handle them, as always in our subject, to the extent that his research methods and his interests allow (Devons and Gluckman 1964).

The disadvantages of a development anthropology which espouses the general perspective of developers are the converse of the alternative's advantages. The development anthropologist must find it difficult to break from the expectation that it is the target group which constitutes his sphere of expertise. Such an expectation is justified to the extent that it is the anthropologist who knows, or can get to know, about the people at the receiving end, but it is nevertheless unfortunate in two particular ways. In the first place, it is based on a definition of the situation which is at odds with the phenomenon to be studied. Development does and must bring into existence social fields, fields of interaction, which span the social and cultural divisions being used to establish spheres of expertise. As a basis for study and prediction, any acceptance of the targets themselves as constituting an isolable social field is counterfactual and severely disabling. This may be felt to apply to the George Foster of *Tzintzuntzan* (1967) and *Applied Anthropology*, with his preoccupation with "cognitive orientations" despite his characterization of the development situation in terms of a "target group", an "innovating organization" and an "interaction setting" (1969). Theory grounded on static assumptions, useful as it may be for some purposes, is necessarily misleading when change and redefinition are at issue.

Secondly, experience strongly suggests that relevance of any knowledge at all of the "target" society is highly variable and cannot be taken for granted. Adams in a seminal article pointed this out long ago and many studies since have confirmed that, to use his words, "the Indians" may be "little more than uncomfortable bystanders in the affair" (Adams 1953 : 11; e.g. Almy 1977 : 286, Apthorpe 1973 : 4, Chambers 1969 and 1975, Charsley 1968, Heginbotham 1975, Mencher 1970, Reining 1966). An advantage of the alternative perspective is that it encourages an open mind on where the practical problems may lie. It also encourages a firm move away from the perceptions so appealing to developers themselves in which explanation is necessarily to be sought in the peculiarities of "the peasants", their "Images of Limited Good", "Amoral Familism", or whatever.

Finally, proper as it may be for the individual anthropologist to espouse the aim of a particular development effort which he knows well, it becomes increasingly perilous for a subject to embrace "development" as a whole. This is not just a matter of the precarious and shifting nature of prevailing definitions but of the increasing awareness of the ambiguous results of development schemes. Even if the benevolence of the rulers and elites who commonly control resources needed for development programmes were assumed, it could not possibly be assumed that their schemes are bound to prove universally beneficent. Some indeed are spectacularly disastrous (cf. Ruddle and Chesterfield 1976). Even where they do not go wrong, are "successful", advantage for some only too often means relative or even absolute disadvantage for others (cf. Epstein 1973, Pt. 2). The weakening of the subsistence base, for instance, does not only offer the opportunity of higher incomes and a greater contribution to national wealth; it also entails greater dependence on national and international markets the vagaries of which, whether controlled or uncontrolled, are far from certain to benefit those who have surrendered their measure of autonomy to them. More generally, increased dependence on towns and industry, and the increased possibilities of control which result, do not necessarily benefit those whom increasing integration has for one reason or another rendered marginal (Adams 1974; Lipton 1977). Finally, to the anthropologist it must be particularly clear that on man's social and cultural "barriers to development" are other people's values. With this increasing awareness, the sceptical observer is more than ever needed.

To be clear : Development is an important phenomenon of the contemporary world and it is one to the study of which anthropologists have a very clear contribution to make. Understanding the phenomenon is important, not only because its potential for good or for ill is great but because understanding can make a difference. It concerns what people do at least as much as what happens to them; choice and decision are prominent, and not only on the developer's side. The understanding in terms of which people act is therefore particularly significant here. It is not that anthropologists should avoid the subject--the opposite rather. What has to be avoided is giving support to that rhetoric in which a development label successfully attached automatically signifies desirability.

A social anthropology of the seeking of improvements can be exemplified by reference to a study of extension in the sericultural industry of Mysore, Karnataka State, South India.[2] This study focuses on the role of the Sericultural Range Officer (SRO), those who play the role and its definition and performance, in order to explain the slightness of achievement. The enterprise is necessarily of some complexity, involving as it necessarily does both first-hand study of the particular instance, and comparison, and generalization from it in relation to practical concerns. What I have room to present here is more an account of the study than the substance of the analysis itself; I am attempting elsewhere to provide in a more extended format a working analysis of development in a number of aspects of sericulture (see also Charsley 1978).

In formal terms the SRO is the person in charge of the lowest-level and smallest of the territorial segments into which the sericultural areas under the jurisdiction of the Sericulture Department of Karnataka State are divided. He is a Class III officer in a typical Indian governmental bureaucracy. His Department is legally charged with the supervision and development of raw-silk production in the State and he is its main instrument in dealing with its charges. His present role as officially defined dates only from 1973 but it has considerable continuity with a past reaching back to the roots of the Department in development activity under the Economic Conference of Mysore before the First World War. The industry itself dates from the end of the 18th century and is entirely the product of experimentation and development since that time (Charsley 1977). What is chiefly apparent about the circulated definition of the role, in eighteen points, is the weakness of any extension or service element in it. It gives pride of place to policing activities in connection with the very considerable legal regulation under which the industry operates and in particular with the issuing of licences and passbooks to rearers. The gathering of statistics and reporting come next, and only after that anything which might be construed as extension: "propaganda", implementing "any development work assigned", and miscellaneous activities such as undertaking "disinfection work as and when necessity arises". Extension's weakness here reflects a high-level preoccupation with the technical transformation of the industry rather than its improvement but, since this depends on resources rarely available in the area concerned, senior officers locally recognize the limited scope for transformation there. The understanding of the SRO's role held by their immediate superiors therefore includes more emphasis on extension and improvement than the document suggests.

SROs in their origins and social identities conform to no single pattern. Though most of those serving in the taluk studied were brought up locally, for only a minority does this mean that they have themselves belonged to village sericultural families. As to caste and religion they are as varied as the population at large : Brahmins and Harijans, Lingayats, Christian and Muslims, as well as the local middle-range castes of some size are all represented. Their economic circumstances are also diverse, a few depending entirely on their salaries for the support of their families but more with some form of access to land and its products in addition. Only rarely do they live actually in their ranges and the main alternative is the local town. But even of those who live in their home villages few can be regarded, or regard themselves, as villagers. They are not dhoti-and-headtowel but shirt-and-trouser, watch-and-attache-case men, clearly marked off from the majority of the population with whom they have to deal.

Their performance of their role tends to be far simpler than its official representation. In their own eyes their main activities are collecting licence fees and inspecting rearings. Collecting statistics and reporting are less burdensome than any real attempt to obtain the required information would make them. Indeed the bias of the official prescription towards policing and reporting is not echoed at all in their own perceptions. Neither however is extension; SROs in general have little sense of being involved in a developing industry at all. Despite their technical training and the regular insistence of their superiors on the defects of current practice, they tend to accept the prevailing assumption among rearers themselves that the current and the proper performance of sericulture are one and the same.

The SRO therefore simplifies his job. In particular he plays down those aspects of it which are likely to generate the hostility of those with whom he must work. He depends upon them to be able to make any showing at all, to provide for him those prepared to take licences, to buy government layings, or who can be persuaded to volunteer for the occasional development 'advantage' he is instructed to provide for them, such as training in new kinds of rearing. Unlike some other extension officers, he has little or nothing in the way of access to valued resources to offer them in return. He has little alternative therefore to tailoring his performance to his clients' expectations. He has at least the advantage that he need worry little about any direct monitoring of his performance; it is carried on in villages which are even less accessible to his superiors than to himself. He does his job, with few exceptions, mainly in the interest of supplying upwards to his superiors the inputs of "information" required of him and of meeting immediate requirements imposed on him such as the selling of licences. His officially assigned tasks are in fact so unmanageable and circumstances so difficult that he could scarcely do otherwise.

Many of the features associated with ineffective extension here are not uncommon. S.C. Dube (1958) and team studied the beginnings of Indian Community Development in North in the mid-1950s; S.J. Heginbotham (1975) studied Agricultural Department staff and Block organization in relation to development in Tamil Nadu in the later 1960s; I am now studying sericulture in another part of the South in the mid-1970s; and there are strong likenesses between the situations reported in these three studies, in many ways so different to one another. The idea of extension in a "Community Development" form (Foster 1969 : 99) is much in evidence, but in practice, far from local needs being identified, policy and often very detailed objectives are generated within the bureaucratic apparatus and handed down for implementation with little apparent sense even of the problems and practicalities of doing so. The distinctive position of the lowest-level field officer, the SRO here, is a further common feature, and the loading on to him, formally at least, of almost everything his superiors, sometimes multifarious, require to get done. With this situation commonly go judgements of lack of success with extension, despite the fact that such a lack is often masked by successful change operating through other, informal, channels.

An explanation of some generality is therefore required. Recourse has traditionally been had to a simple dichotomous view : those involved are either developers or targets. The former can be assumed to have what the latter need and to be active in putting it over to them. That the latter do not take what is offered must show that something is wrong with them, making them resistant. They are conservative, tradition-bound, primitive, suffer from false consciousness, or whatever. It is a perspective which, as I have noted, inevitably appeals to developers themselves, though they may be humanly sympathetic with the people's misguidedness, or even feel a nostalgia for what they imagine to be the way of life they are engaged in sweeping away. They may even employ an anthropologist to advise on the people's quirks and ways of getting round them.

Dube's study in the 1950s was marked by such a perspective. When he deals with "Problems of Communication" these are essentially between the development apparatus as a whole and the villagers. His "Cultural Factors in Community Development" are all aspects of village culture : *their* habits and taste, social practices and tradition, beliefs, social structure, attitudes and values. Yet he includes also a crucial chapter on "State Officials as Agents of Change" and an appendix on the role of the Village Level Worker. The effect of his study was therefore to begin to undermine the simple dichotomous strategy. First-hand experience, even in show-villages in the first eighteen months of a great new departure, compelled recognition of the need to take the apparatus and its problems into account and made it unavoidably clear that outcomes are not adequately represented as either acceptance or rejection of what is proposed. The process is a far more complex and dynamic one, involving review, consideration, choice and adaptation, and this is a fundamental discovery for any social anthropology of development.

Such an approach still however takes the setting of development goals and their presentation to those to be developed very much for granted, as if they were irrelevant to outcomes. It is by now clear, as was pointed out in the first part of this essay, that the main problems may often lie in this very area. Heginbotham's contribution is to have concentrated attention on the bureaucracy itself. He brings to the explanation a self-conscious theory, the theory that is the interplay of contrasting cognitive orientations which gives rise to an immobilization of the apparatus. A system designed to maximize the effectiveness and control of the top, formerly British, staff and to minimize the scope for deviation on the part of the juniors has had added to it a "dharmic" perception of duty. This is seen as a matter of doing what is formally required of one by authority, without any further considerations as to utility or even practicability. This leads, according to him, to a situation in which goals are determined, targets set, quite independent of any considerations of implementation, in which requirements are simply handed down the hierarchy, the superior at each stage being concerned only to extract work from his subordinates, i.e. evidence of whatever kind that requirements are being met, which can then be passed back up the chain. The crunch comes at the bottom where the lowest level of officer has no-one from whom he in turn can extract work. On him rest all his superiors' possibilities of being seen to be doing their duties.

But this officer's predicament is not simply the resulting overload; it if formed also by a conflict at this level between the further cognitive models and those already in action. Heginbotham's lowest-level officers are trained under Community Development and to some extent Gandhian perspectives and there is therefore for them a conflict between, on the one side, meeting the expectations of superiors and doing their dharmic duty, and, on the other, its antithesis, discovering local needs and feeding requirements and ideas into the apparatus with a view to it then solving local problems. "The result was not simply a routinization of procedure, but a severe and progressive deterioration of performance, integrity and morale" (1975 : 122).

However, he seems here too be seeking too specific an explanation for the generality of the phenomenon. With none of his cognitive orientations much in evidence in the Sericulture Department, and certainly to conflict between any Community Development trained field staff and traditionally minded superiors, the results were much the same. It seems to me that one must go back to an old anthropological theme of great generality, i.e. to the recognition of the Village Level Worker, the Gram Sevak, the SRO as intercalary roles (Gluckman 1949 ; Fallers 1965 : 196 foll.). That is to say, they are roles which stand between radically separate and unequal sections of society and have their nature defined by their intermediary position. For simplicity I return to the SRO, the role that I know best. Intercalary roles may take a variety of forms depending on their performers' identities for the sides between which they mediate, but it is crucial to the understanding of the SRO, I suggest, that he belongs fully to neither of the sections he stands between. As a salaried government servant, an 'officer', he is marked off from the society of those with whom it is his duty to work. He is neither seen or generally sees himself as belonging to village society. Indeed by dress and accoutrements he marks himself off visibly from it. Yet he is also firmly marked off from all but the most junior of those who are formally his colleagues in the Sericulture Department (cf. Mook 1974 : 148 and passim). They, as graduates with superior technical training and prospects of promotion, with their offices and subordinate staffs, belong in actuality or in aspiration to the city-based, non-traditional middle class. Individually, they are not necessarily without connections into village society ; a few indeed are the sons of village sericultural families. But even such people are separated from their origins by their own educational, occupational and social advancement. SROs however are immobilized between the two. Members of the small-town salariat, they are more likely to slip into, or back into, the rural, farming society than ever to move firmly into the urban middle-class world (cf. Mencher 1970 : 1188). Between the apparatus and the clients, between the middle class and the village stands the SRO, and little can be understood of his position and problems unless that is grasped.

It is necessary in the first place to the understanding of his weakness as a link. It is not just that he is at the bottom of a bureaucratic chain, though this already makes any two-way flow of information difficult. It is that he is separated from the chain, not fully a part of it. His involvement with the village world indicates his inferiority to his superiors, an inferiority which villagers of higher status are not slow to perceive (Dube 1958 : 177). Yet such a person is expected to be the bureaucracy's ambassador, representative and instruments in its dealings with the village world (Mencher 1970 : 1191/2).

It is necessary secondly for an understanding of why so many tasks get directed, and so unrealistically, towards the SRO. Such a role is required, indeed produced, precisely by the disjunction between the middle-class world of the apparatus and the village world deemed inferior. As far as the lack of realism is concerned, superiority of position makes for assured superiority of knowledge and perception, and the precarious field officer is in no position to challenge this through any questioning of the requirements presented to him. He generates no feedback which might provide a check on superior misconceptions (Mencher 1970 : 1192). But perhaps more important than any real lack of knowledge of what goes on in the village world—for sericultural officers are practical men in their outlooks and, as I have noted, do sometimes have direct village links—is the devaluing of such knowledge implicit in this kind of sharply satisfied social structure. As P.K.B. Nayar puts it in discussing the communication gap between the bureaucracy and the people : "The bureaucrat belongs to a culture different from the majority of his clients who are illiterate and superstitious villagers" (1975-183).

The issue of rearing houses exemplifies this. Financial provision for such buildings appears in each new programme of development. There are technical reasons why separate houses might be superior but, despite years of encouragement, virtually none have been constructed. The reasons are not far to seek : rearing is carried on within dwelling houses which are in this area reasonably suited structurally to it, and practices are in adjustment with this location. The work is undertaken quite largely by women of respectable village families who find little difficulty in carrying it out within their own homes, in particular the feeding at intervals during the night which the young worms are deemed to require. The same procedure could be less readily followed in separate houses. Such buildings therefore offer benefits which are unproven, at a cost which reaches even beyond the cost and trouble of constructing them to an awkward reorganization of established rearing practices. It is scarcely surprising that there is no interest in this policy amongst sericulturists, yet official enthusiasm for it continues undaunted. It is not that those responsible for such policies do not know in any absolute sense of such practical considerations ; it is rather, I suggest, that such village knowledge is devalued relative to their own technical knowledge.

Furthermore, as middle-class officers the higher ranks have no effective access to the village world. As Mook (1974 : 137 foll.) makes clear in the case of Agricultural Officers, this applies even to the lowest graduate rank, here the Circle Officer, and the plea of excessive office work keeping them out of the field is by no means the full story. Officers of all ranks may indeed visit villages occasionally, even, touring in the old British tradition, but then, as important and rare visitors, they necessarily disrupt the flow of life around them. They communicate with others, most often of course with village leaders and so-called middle-class farmers (Mencher 1970 : 1192), in a specialized, not to say artificial context (cf. Chambers 1975 :3). They do not move in rural areas without an entourage of subordinates, and they generally appear and disappear in motor vehicles. They normally receive the deference of village people which they are likely to take, not always justifiably perhaps, as signifying respect. SROs by contrast move unattended, on foot or by bicycle, exciting a minimum of attention.

But to get anything done, even to find out anything on a systematic basis, the superior officer is largely helpless. He requires the lowly SRO since he is the only one who is able and above all willing to spend time travelling around villages and in the company of villagers, things that the educated person of higher class is by and large unwilling to do. He is the only one who knows who people are and how to find them. Superiors in such a divided society have therefore no alternative to handing field tasks, whatever they may be, to such officers. Together with the devaluation of what knowledge is available of the village circumstances under which the SRO must operate, it is this which accounts for the magnitude and unreality of the prescribed role.

Finally, and crucial to the extension problem, is the fact that this prescribed role is only indirectly observable by superiors. In practice they may monitor and control formal outputs but scarcely field performance. That, the aspect of the role intended to have causal efficacy in promoting development, is controlled to a far greater extent by those with whom the SRO must work, the village sericulturists. Almost every lowest-level field officer is faced therefore with reconciling conflicting requirements and producing a performance which is viable in relation to them. There thus arises the marked difference often observed between the formal prescription and the role as performed. I have noted the way the task in sericulture is simplified and formalized. Heginbotham finds his "heavily burdened Gram Sevak" (1975 : 164) by "great irony" underworked and not knowing what to do with himself in his villages (183/4). The weakness of the SRO's position, and the positions of other lowest-level field officers, is such, I am suggesting, that he can perform an extension role only when this is actually required of him by his clients. In the area studied it was not.

This then is a small example of the style of social anthropology of development that I am advocating. It attempts an open-minded analysis of the processes set up by attempts at development. Success (e.g. Baviskar 1978) is as much grist to its mill as difficulties, though the latter more clearly provide both focus and incentive for analysis. It analyses the individual case and seeks the more general in it. The discussion presented here, I may note, moves from sericulture in Mysore to Indian extension more generally. It could undoubtedly be extended still further, since similar situation may be expected rather generally in post-colonial societies (cf. Chambers 1975). Wherever a disjunction develops between the rural and the urban, the peasant and the intelligensia, similar extension difficulties are likely to follow. I contend that such studies have a practical as well as a theoretical use. Though they do not tell anyone what to do, they do raise the issues which form essential starting points for future planning. They contribute an important element to the available experience without which schemes repeatedly founder on the same uncharted reefs.

NOTES

1. But the "anthropology" to which he refers is very differently conceived and the project becomes both vaguer and more grandiose than this single quotation suggests.
2. Research on the silk industry was carried out throughout 1975, mainly in Kollegal Taluk, Mysore. The present tense in description refers to that date. The study was financed by the British S.S.R.C., to whom grateful acknowledgement is made. Thanks are also due to the Director of Sericulture and the many members of his staff who assisted me in all possible ways.

SUGGESTED READINGS

Adams, R.N., "Notes on the Application of Anthropology," *Hum. Organization 12*, 2, 1953, 10-14.

Adams, R.N., Harnessing Technological Development, in Poggie, J.J. and Lynch, R.N. (eds.), *Rethinking Modernization*. Westport (Conn.); Greenwood Press, 1974.

Almy, S.W., Anthropologists and Development Agencies, *Am. Anth. 79*, 2, 1977.

Apthorpe, R., Peasants and Planistrators in Eastern Africa 1960-70, Conference paper, ASA Oxford, 1973.

Barnett, T., *The Gezira Scheme : An Illusion of Development*, London : Cass, 1977.

Bastide, R., *Applied Anthropology*, London : Croom Helm, 1973.

Baviskar, B.S., "Making Co-operatives a Success : An Anthropologist's View", Conference paper, SSRC Workshop on the Anthropology of Economic Development. University of Sussex, 1978.

Belshaw, C.S., Anthropology and Development Studies, *Int Soc. Sci. J. XXIV*, 1, 1972, 80-94.

Chambers, R , *Settlement Schemes in Tropical Africa*, London : Routledge 1969.

Chambers, R., *Two Frontiers in Rural Management*, Communication No. 113, Brighton : IDS, 1975.

Charsley, S.R., "The Group Farm Scheme in Uganda", in Apthorpe, R. (ed.) *Land Settlement and Rural Development in Eastern Africa*, Nkanga No. 3, Kampala : Transition Books, 1968.

Charsley, S.R., "Silk Production in Karnataka : An Outline History", *Indian Silk XVI*, 4, 1977, 7-12.

Charsley, S.R., "Agricultural Extension and its Problems in India : The Case of the Sericultural Range Officer of Mysore", Conference paper, SSRC Workshop on the Anthropology of Economic Development, University of Sussex, 1978.

Copans, J. and Seddon, D., "Marxism and Anthropology : A Preliminary Survey", in Seddon, D., (ed). *Relation of Production.*, London : Cass, 1978.

Dalton, G., *Economic Anthropology and Development*, New York : Basic Books, 1971.

Devons, E. and GLUCKMAN, M., Conclusions, *Closed Systems and Open Minds*, Edinburgh : Oliver and Boyd, 1964.

Dube, S.C., *India's Changing Villages*, London : Routledge, 1958.

Epstein, T.S., *South India : Yesterday, Today and Tomorrow*, London : Macmillan, 1973.

Firth, R., The Sceptical Anthropologist ? Social Anthropology and Marxist Views on Society, in Bloch, M. (ed.) *Marxist Analyses and Social Anthropology*, London : Malaby Press, 1975.

Fallers, L.A., *Bantu Bureaucracy*, Chicago : University of Chicago Press, 1965. (First edition 1956, Cambridge : Heffer, for E.A.I.S.R)

Foster, G.M., *Tzintzuntzan : Mexican Peasants in a Changing World*, Boston : Little, Brown, 1967.

Foster, G.M., *Applied Anthropology*, Boston : Little, Brown, 1969.

Foster-Carter, A., Neo-Marxist Approaches to Development and Under-development, in de Kadt, E. and Williams, G. (eds.) *Sociology and Development*, London : Tavistock, 1974.

Gluckman, M., The Village Headmen in British Central Africa, *Africa XIX*, 1949.

Heginbotham, S.J., *Cultures in Conflict : The Four Faces of India's Bureaucracy*, New York : Columbia U.P, 1975.

Lipton, M., *Why Poor People Stay Poor : A Study of Urban Bias in World Development*, London : Temple Smith, 1977.

Mair, L., "Applied Anthropology and Development Policies", *British J. Social 7*, Reprinted in her *Anthropology and Social Change*, London : Athlone Press, 1956.

Mead, M., "Changing Perspectives on Modernization", in Poggie, J.J. and Lynch, R.N. (eds.) *Rethinking Modernization*, Westport (Conn) : Greenwood Press, 1974.

Meadows, D.H., *et.al.*, *The Limits to Growth : A Report for the Club of Rome's Project on the Predicament of Mankind*, London : Earth Island, 1972.

Mencher, J.P., Change Agents and Villagers, *Econ. and Polit. Weekly* : 1970, 1187-97.

Mook, B.T., *Value and Action in Indian Bureaucracy*, Discussion Paper 65, Brighton : IDS, 1974.

Nayar, P.K.B. "Administrative Context of Economic Development", in Nair., B.N. (ed.) *Culture and Society*, Delhi : Thomson Press, 1975.

Oshima, H.T., "New Directions in DevelopmentS trategies", *Econ. Dev. and Cult. Change 25*, 3, 1977.

Poggie, J.J. and Lynch, R.N. (eds.) *Rethinking Modernization : Anthropological Perspectives*, Westport (Conn.) : Greenwood Press, 1974.

Reining, C., *The Zande Scheme : An Anthropological Study of Economic Development in Africa*, Evanston : Northwestern U.P., 1966.

Ruddle, K. and Chesterfield, R., "Change Perceived as Man-made Hazard in a Rural Development Environment", *Dev. and Change 7*, 1976.

Sachs, I., "The Logic of Development," *Int. Soc. Sci J. XXIV*, 1, 1972.

Seers, D., What are We Trying to Measure ? *J. Dev. Studies 8*, 3, 1972.

Terray, E., *Marxism and "Primitive Societies"*, New York : Monthly Review Press, 1972.

FIVE

Jacques Lombard

FRENCH ANTHROPOLOGY AFTER THE SIXTIES

A Determinist Renewal ?

IN 1960, on the eve of the independence of African countries, French ethnology way characterized by a number of trends, mainly archaeological researches, the development of monographic surveys on ethnic groups, and the elucidation of mythical and religious thought, especially by Griaule.

At the same time, ethnology tended to become more sociological under the influence of Gurvitch and Balandier and also more "anthropological", in the sense Lévi-Strauss used the word, taking up the point of view of Kroeber.

The independence of African countries was to put an end to classical ethnology, challenged by the new generation of anthropologists who were to denounce its collusion with colonialism.

The urgency of the development of the Third World and the scientific inadequacies of a discipline which was considered as too empirical and not historical enough were to direct French anthropology toward the study of economic phenomena in a Marxist prospect, especially after the publication in French of *Ancient Society* by Morgan, and of the *Forms that Precede Capitalist Production* by Marx. The student movements of May, 1968, in France were also relevant to this change of direction.

These last two decades have brought the development of an anthropology which either is integrated to an interdisciplinary reflection related to development, or is more fundamentally aims at the reconstitution of precapitalist economic systems.

But this determinist renewal is likely to come across limitations somewhat similar to those evolutionism had known, when it was condemned by functionalism. A few examples of critical significance are given of this.

French Anthropology after the Sixties : A Determinist Renewal ?

In 1956, on the eve of the independence of African countries, a sociological review published in France attempted to situate ethnology in this country. The author recorded a certain number of trends, some of them already of long standing, others more recent.[1]

Among the oldest trends, he recorded that some researches associated to prehistory and archaeology, illustrated in Europe by Leroi-Gourhan, in Asia by Mus, and in America by Soustelle, were going on. French ethnology was also characterized by the multiplication of studies centered on the description and the analysis (often in the form of a monographs) of still hardly-known societies. These studies followed the tradition born in the thirties under the impulse of Malinowski, Radcliffe-Brown and other British and French researchers. This field work aimed at increasing the still far too incomplete information about so-called "primitive" peoples. Another trend consisted in intensive research applied to a more specialized theme, such as the knowledge of myths and religion, studies in which Griaule and Leenhardt prevailed. A last trend, represented by Bastide, investigated, in a more general and also more sociological view-point, wider fields such as the encounter of civilizations and other subjects that interrelate ethnology and sociology, on the one hand, and psychology and psychoanalysis on the other.

These last two tendencies were to mark, right after the Second World War, a certain renewal of the French school, and at the same time a clear cut within it between an increasingly sociological direction, inspired by Bastide and Balandier, under the influence of Gurvitch, and an anthropological and structuralist direction, led by Lévi-Strauss. Traditional ethnology was coming to an end in 1959 with the disappearance of so-called "primitive" societies on the way to a fast modernization, to give way to a sociology of societies that were still "different" but more and more confronted by the problems of the Western world ; or else to reappear as a more component of a new anthropology whose purpose was the ambitious, but fascinating, study of all the present and past societies, according to the definition given by Levi-Strauss, which was close to the conceptions Kroeber had put forward in *Anthropology Today*.

Differing in the objective, these two directions also were to diverge in their methods, one giving a predominant place to history and conflict, and the other one looking for invariants and structures beyond time and space. But neither of the two seemed able to lead to really scientific generalizations, and each tended to restrict itself to areas in which its approaches were most rewarding : that of politics and change, for the one, and that of parental relationship and myth for the other. The first one was founded on Gurvitch's fertile views, insisting on the necessity of a global approach, and on the precariousness of any social structure in a constantly renewing reality, marked by conflicts and inequalities: it also accepted as its own Gluckman's conception of dynamic anthropology, and to a certain extent that of Leach. The second direction, more serene and less "contingent", led to too general an explanation to be truly explanatory; it valued greatly some tendencies of social behaviour, such as the necessity of exchange and reciprocity as fundamental elements of social communication. However, it was too general an explanation, perhaps, and essentially psychological any way.

The years that followed the independences were also those when French ethnology, especially with the emergence of a young generation of researchers, became less associated with the colonialism; yet it had to face a double crisis: a crisis concerning the very foundations of a discipline that no longer appeared as innocent, and seemed to have no future because of the transformations of its object; and, secondly, a crisis born of the dissatisfaction felt about its scientific inadequacies.

Taking up the themes of the American, Gough, a group of anthropologists, and especially Copans, denounced the historically close association between anthropology and imperialism.[2] Gough had asserted that anthropology was the daughter of imperialism. Rightly enough, an ideological function of "rationalization" and "scientificity" of colonial practices was ascribed to it. In addition to its role of challenging the colonial phenomenon anthropology, with the rehabilitation of dominated cultures. (especially African ones) had furthered the cause of the first nationalist movements trying to revalourize the historical and cultural patrimony of dependent societies, and its responsibility was clear nonetheless.

Evolutionism had favoured the first colonial expeditions, justifying a political intervention into societies whose stage of evolution was still far from reaching that of European populations, hence the necessity of a colonization which brought peace and civilization. Later on, at the time of the zenith of Western domination, functionalism was to "idealize" the colonial presence by hiding anthropology disturbing role and the conflicts it aroused. It valourized all the social mechanism meant to maintain the balance and harmony of societies, even those which were more dominated by foreign cultures. One recalls the famous theses of Malinowski in *The Dynamics Culture Change*, optimistic theses in which colonization brought a new culture, harmoniously born of the gradual adjustment of the cultures in contact. That was also the time when field research increased substantially, as well as the study of topics having a practical application, whether economic or administrative.

The internal contestation of anthropology by anthropologists was not only the product of the collective remorse of a generation toward the past of a science whose heritage was theirs; it also came from the feeling that the object of study had changed. Opening to sociology and research on conflicts and inequalities, research was to give up studying disappearing small communities such as villages or tribes in order to tackle, on a wider scale, national formations and states, which were gradually consolidating. Together with the "primitive" also declined the monographic survey on a village or a tribe, the investigation of isolated communities, and a whole discipline that had become, through fieldwork and the ideology of its doctrines, the auxiliary of an obsolete colonial situation which was now denounced.

Less known and not so well-explained as this political constestation, the "scientific" crisis of anthropology nonetheless existed. After a century of existence, the discipline had not asserted itself as a science; it did not seem to have answered the expectations of the "founding fathers," who had believed in the possibility of explaining human behaviour by universal laws. As years went by, their ambitions had become more modest, and the fundamental problem of the status of anthropology, whether as a science or as a "literary" discipline—a problem which was well illustrated at a few years' interval by the respective positions of Radcliffe-Brown and Evans-Pritchard, who had become skeptical toward the advent of an anthropological science—went together with a number of dilemmas inwhich the researchers inevitably locked themselves. If anthropology really was a science, its vocation was to discover a set of universal laws, revealing common phenomena in humanity, whatever societies fashioned people. But at the same time, it admitted a certain determinism in the structures and a constraining social frame that minimized men's individual variations and their possibilities of free reaction. If, on the contrary, it restricted itself to remain only the "science" of "different" societies, it then gave up any claim to universality, reinforced its relativist orientation, and valourized a particularist explanation specific to the society studied. Thus, it privileged the human dimension, the possibilities of variation due to the role of the individual or some particular groups, it granted to social agents capacities of initiative and control in the process of social change.

This dilemma was very well stated by Levi-Strauss, who was confident of the virtues of anthropology to overcome its own contradictions. He postulates that if anthropology is the science of the differences and specificities of cultures, these differences are complementary and must lead to the discovery of universals in the permanent mental structures common to all cultures. But the question arises, whether one can solve such an important contradiction, largely illustrated by the ethnological production, by going beyond it to such a general and abstract level ?

The search for universals always works by a process of reduction, the reduction of complex facts to a number of fixed or minimally variable elements. In a first stage, societal diversity was reduced by evolutionists to a number of "types" fashioned by economic and social conditions, and all, through history each society was supposed to have gone through stages or types. Diffusionism reduced all the "different" societies to the cultural elements that composed them and to the geographic origins of their diffusion. As for the functionalist reduction, it consisted in explaining cultures, not through their origins or their determining factors, but through a limited set of functions to which corresponded the main institutions.

All these schools led to explanations that were too general or too common to be really scientific. Moreover, as they tried to insist more on what unified than separated, they often tended to become ethnocentric and interpret the phenomena they observed by referring to patterns attached to the society of the Western observer. Must the nature-culture pattren (although of universal character or considered as such) be considered as proper to all societies and to the representations they have of this pattern, or on the contrary, must it be considered as that of a certain Western logic at a given period ? In connection with this, one will remember the famous economic rationality of the classical economists, who had determined its criteria, then considered it to be universal and unchangeable; later, however, this was rejected by anthropologists.

The researchers' dissatisfaction with the mediocrity of the results obtained by the attempts at scientific generalizations leed some to a less ambitious but more realistic view of the anthropological project. A more relativistic conception incited them to consider any culture as specific and irreducible to any other. Techniques, organizations, mentalities, and values were to be considered as a whole, and this whole could only be explained in itself, as each institution was coherent only in relation to this whole. It tended to exclude any attempt at analogies and comparisons with other societies, and, as a consequence, any generalization. This position was to some extent that of the American cultural anthropology, and of BOAS in particular, whose mistrust in any universal explanation was well-known. Most of all, it was the position of Evans-Pritchard, who gave to anthropology the vocation to search for "structures and not laws", to demonstrate "the coherence of phenomena and not the existence of necessary relations between social activities".

This view was that of most anthropologists in the second half of the twentieth century and during the final years of colonialism, if one excepts the ambitious structuralist project.

It is with this view that monographs and the above-mentioned privileged study of the ethnic group, considered as unit of investigation, began to be written. This view also divided the anthropological universe into diverse specialities, which often defined themselves more on geographic bases than on common themes.

As it turned into a discipline of erudition—more and more divided as the studies progressively multiplied in each continent and cultural area—and as the knowledge of peoples became more and more differentiated, anthropology was condemned for the failure of its "primitive" scientific focus and for the mere accumulation, without explanation, of knowledge that had only helped to serve the interests of colonial powers.

Thus, after the 1960s, French anthropology found itself dominated by two schools of thought: one was more sociological than ethnological, stressing the importance of history, conflict, and inequalitarian relations, and rejecting the research of "primitives" and any participation (even an unconscious one) in a colonial past ; the other school was more anthropological and universal, but also was more detached from contemporary historical reality.

On the other hand, French anthropology benefited from an anthropological history that was beginning to be better-known through the multiplication of translations from British and American authors, and through a closer contact with them. This history revealed the crisis of a science, which was unable to explain and even more to generalize, as it was imprisoned in the double contradiction between an impossible universalist explanation and a necessary respect of multiple specific realities.

One first reaction of the researchers, as well as those to whom they transmitted their knowledge, was to "send back home" the old exotic ethnology, just as their representatives had been sent home at the end of the colonialism, and to apply to Western countries those elements of ethnological experience which were considered to be positive. The study of African, American, or Eastern cultures was to be left to the initiative of the representatives of the new nations. But the necessities of an urgent development of these nations—in an international frame which was more and more interdependent, in spite of a more unobtrusive but just as real Western domination—stimulated economic reflection and made concerted action necessary. Economics, then, was to stimulate research, and it invaded such varied areas as history, geography, and even anthropology. Within this new focus centered upon the development of the Third World, all the disciplines, each in its speciality, focused their researches on economic subjects.

The new French anthropology tried to renew its themes, even though some earlier trends of research continued to exist: in the field of parental relationship, around Levi-Strauss; in political anthropology, following the British tradition of research; and, lastly concerning social change. In the last of these, particularly around Balandier, sociology looked away from the old ethnology and directed its attention toward processes of modernization: rural development, migration, and urbanization. All the young generation of researchers who still had the possibility to study on the field, including anthropologists of the new national states, whether African or not, could witness the first great economic and social transformation after independence was attained. It is not surprising that, among the new themes, economics was most often selected by this new sociologizing anthropology; and within it, the prevailing study of modern phenomena posed no obstacle to referring as much as possible, in a historical approach, to more ancient facts from pre-colonial societies.

And yet, the reoriented anthropology was soon to show itself more ambitious and once more it become preoccupied with more fundamental research. Classical anthropology had been accused of being too descriptive and too monographical during the last years of the colonialism; many regretted the lack of really scientific problematics and also too "empirical" trend born with structural-functionalism. The new interest in history gave new life and interest to the old evolutionist problematics, although they were deprived of their racist and imperialist ideology. Suddenly the long tradition born with Malinowski, which had been revolutionary in its time, appeared to be a parenthesis in the history of anthropology, a parenthesis essentially characterized by the renunciation of the historical and evolutionary approaches. Malinowski was remembered as a man of the field, but researches now did not mind going back to the great questions of conjectural history that he had expelled from anthropology. Hence, the model became Morgan, a man of the field too, but whose conclusions had largely gone beyond the restricted circle of a Melanesian archipelago and, what is more, were akin to those of Marx and Engels. As occurred with the neo-evolutionism of Leslie White, a new Marxist anthropology, but with a very different outlook, took over from the oldest anthropological school; it examined the old "primitive" societies and their modes of production, as well as the processes of penetration of commercial economy into pre-capitalist systems, making use of observations this time. This movement was conditionedby several events. First, Morgan's *Ancient Society* finally (1971) was translated into French, almost a century after it had been published in the U.S.A.; such a delay does not appear to be unintentional, as it probably results from the influence of functionalist anthropology, which was conservative and linked to colonial powers. Second, this work converged with that of Engels, whose *Origins of the Family, Private Property, and the State*, inspired by Morgan's, was already well-known. The May 1968 events in France generated the questioning of several taboos and values which until then were considered to be universal, such as the anteriority of the domestic family to the extended family and the clan, a point of view which was eagerly defended by Malinowski and rejected by Morgan. The family, considered sacred by a whole Judeo-Christian tradition, became with Morgan the "superstructural" product of a new economic stage linked to the advent of private property. The state, as well, was condemned, since it appeared to be the source of individual and possibly autocratic power, compared to what pre-state democratic societies (such as the Iroquois) had known, i.e., being organized around a system of collegial participation in power, and having no property except collective property of the means of production. The last event was the discovery, and the translation into French, of some of Marx's manuscripts, such as *The Forms that Precede Capitalist Production*. This stimulated Marxist anthropological research toward the discovery of the modes of production of the societies it studied; but this discovery was accompanied by a desire to read Marx again, with the liberal spirit born in 1968, and without any interpretation influenced whatsoever by the official exegesis of a political apparatus. Thus, the new French anthropology revolves around two overlapping axes: more fundamentalist one, looking for precapitalist modes of production in self sufficing economies, as well as in societies with an embryonic state (around, for example, the Asiatic mode of production and non-Western situations of feudality); another axis is more involved in research on the development and transformation of economic and social structures—themes that require from ethno-sociologist closer collaboration with economists, geographers, and historians interested in relations of domination. Everywhere prevails research, using explanations by economic factors, as well as the analysis of old and new forms of exploitation.

Whether we consider economists such as Amin, historians as Coquery-Vidrovitch, or sociologists working around Meillassoux, the common field remains Africa, and the themes of research crystallize around imperialism and relations between nations, the development of capitalism and concurrently of social classes, economic changes in rural areas and the new social differentiations that come from them, and the movements of population linked to the growth of wage labour and the growth of towns. At last, the past colonial exploitation is being analysed in terms of the handicaps which new nations confront in their development.

"Fundamentalist" anthropology has turned more deliberately to past systems and undertaken more ambitious and systematic studies of precapitalist economies. The most revealing project of this ambitious approach is that of Godelier who, inspired at the same time by the structuralism of Lévi-Strauss and by Marxism, gives as an object to economic anthropology "the theoretical comparative analysis of the different existing and possible economic systems", thus agreeing with the meaning that Levi-Strauss gives to anthropology. Beyond the particular formal pattern of economic systems, the anthropologist must seek to find "common formal patterns" (constants) in all societies, through the study of all past, present, and imaginable economic systems. This structuralist attitude, also characterized by the search for a hidden logic and for unintentional properties of social structures, went together with a Marxist and historical orientation; and as the years went by, it was to assert itself more vigorously than the previous one of "analyzing the determining role of economy in the last instance, according to the modes of production, the historical periods and the prevailing role of social structures", to which Godelier attaches great importance.

This is a difficult project to realize because of both the level of abstraction to which it tries to situate the generalization, and because of this work has become almost impossible due to the rapid disappearance of precapitalist systems and thus the possibilities of observing them. The search for the constitutive characters of the "Asiatic mode of production," to which this author applied himself after considering some elements given by Marx about this precapitalist model, shows both the interest in such an analysis and the limits to which it leads, since there exists no present system of reference whatsoever.

The anthropological and economic project of Meillassoux undoubtedly appears as more realizeable, as it limits itself to the African continent, in its sub-Saharan part and as it aims at the reconstitution of a series of systems of economies from the self-sufficing ones, to the merchant economies, as well as the "predatory", slave systems and those with a sovereign monopoly. This project comes up to some expectations that no doubt, were not exclusively, French for concurrently in the U.S.A., the school of Polanyi had filled a few gaps, in particular the study of a functioning economy organized around a monarchic regime.[3] All these studies on the precapitalist modes of production, as well as on the penetration of merchant economy into traditional economies, have led to a great number of publications, a synthesis of which is in the course of preparation.

The fact remains that any synthesis and attempt at generalization are likely to come up against two types of difficulties. One is classical : it is the result of too great a haste to generalize from only one or two studies. For instance, it is difficult to define the characteristics of a system of self-sufficing economy and apply them to pastoral societies, based on the investigation of one or two agricultural economies. Their relations of production, confirming to those of parental relationship, are of different nature—at least in the African societies—and are less prevalent in the former than in the latter. The second difficulty is more technical and applies to all the economic researches in anthropology. One cannot indeed study an economy without quantitative data, and it is obvious that if the information collected can reveal the presence or absence of certain institutions, and their role and how they work, it cannot give with precision the importance of production or economic transfers. So then, how can we define the part taken by a "predatory" or a "slave" activity in a traditional economy, otherwise founded on self-sufficiency, if one cannot approximately estimate the importance of the tribute given by a dominated group, or the percentage of men submitting to a servile regime ?

To these obstacles another criticism is added ; this criticism is not new, and it applies to any attempt at "universalist" generalization. The risk of ethnocentrism is present everywhere, and attempts to assimilate the forms of opposition in these types of economy to patterns found in capitalist society raise obvious difficulties. Conflicts between groups evoke an embryonic class struggle, even though these groups are characterized by fluidity in their composition and can change according to situations. Western concepts often become too restraining.

We shall not insist on the common remark that the economic factor is not always prevalent, for as Salisbury has shown about the Siane, an increase of productive forces does not always modify the level of production (at least in the short term), since traditional ideology can play a major role in showing down production. Rather, one must be aware of the difficulties aroused by a radically determinist explanation which makes people and their capacities to react disappear from the social field. As the late Clastres recently wrote, "Primitive society is not the passive plaything of the blind game of productive forces"[4] ; and quite often the "economist" approach gives too mechanical a vision, tending to view persons as passively undergoing the exploitation of a ruling group power of initiative and success is faultless. In "traditional" societies, as well as in the modern context, rivalry between lineages disappears to the benefit of the objective alliance of the elders, as against their descendants, the "youngers." In the modern context, similarly, the capitalist forces in the periphery plan in advance the importance of migratory flux, drawing from traditional economies to supply labourers and commodities cheaply to the developing merchant economy.

Although the hypothesis is attractive and the explanation partly supported both examples forget the role played by other factors, above all the power of initiative and reaction of people who have increasingly become influenced greatly by forces beyond their locale or control.

In sum, these remarks suggest that today a double contradiction is apparent within French anthropology. The first one lies within the dynamist school, which originated with the sociologist, Gurvitch, and the anthropologist, Balandier. The former had insisted that the forces of change in any social organization were continually being structured and de-structured, the latter concerning Black Africa especially ; and in an equally dynamic and inequalitarian outlook on social relations, he emphasized the capacities of resistance, reaction, and even innovation among individuals and oppressed groups in colonial situations. In this conflictual and inequalitarian perspective, people retained power in history, and manifested a capacity for resisting forces that were not always as homogeneous or monolithic as they appeared at first sight. Too mechanical a Marxist approach may very well take up this old outlook again, giving a large role to "individual variations" in social change.

The second contradiction concerns an inadequacy between the method and the object. One of the consequences of the disappearance of political imperialism was the "repatriation" of classical, culturally-inclined ethnology. The gradual decrease of research in non-Western areas incited many to consider a reorientation of anthropology toward Western locations. This attempt is not new, incidentally. It had already been outlined by Firth, who insisted that the field of anthropology was wider than that of "primitive" or small-sized societies, and concerned rural and even industrial societies as well.[5] Anthropology in the Western societies thus showed its specificity not so much through its object, as it applied to any type of community, but rather through its techniques and its approach, which were based more upon observation and interviews than upon quantitative analyses.

To a certain extent this anthropology renews sociology by stressing the psychological dimension, actual experiences rather than mental or jural norms, and the study of minorities in relation to majority trends or "average profiles" as revealed by questionnaires, i.e. minorities in sections of towns, gangs, and other marginal groups.

Paradoxically, in more remote locations the very same anthropology wanted to become economic, and anthropology there associated itself with a science necessarily more and more characterized by statistics. But, as we have seen, qualitative anthropology can hardly satisfy the demands of reconstruction of old economic systems and their modes of production, for lack of quantitative references.

Together with this contradiction, here lie the risk and the handicap that surround the future of French research in economic anthropology. This suggests that again the future way remains narrow, between an orientation toward a determinist science of a universal character and an orientation toward generalization in a more modest and particularist frame. It may matter less whether anthropology meets all the characteristics of a "true" science if it can fulfil the expectations of its time. In a world which tends toward standardization and which, both in the past and present, searches for the values and the fundamental institutions that have been and will always be necessary to it, the fundamental question may be of a totally different nature.

For a hundred years anthropology had contributed to revealing the relativity of several values which, to our eyes, seemed universal. It has shown the close relation between some of them with historical situations or economic standards of development, and thus, it has raised the questionof the permanence or contingency of social and cultural phenomenon. Without undertaking to discover the laws of historical change, or those which rule the behaviour of an individual or a group, would it not be possible for anthropology to look within "different" societies for the answers to problems whose university is revealed by their performance throughout time? The data exist. It would be sufficient to augment them and to systematize their analysis. Some "invariants", then, appear more differentiated than those resulting from the organicist investigations of classical functionalism, and more concrete than those brought by the newer structuralists.

NOTES

1. G. Balandier, Tendences de l'ethnologie française, *Cahiers internationaux de sociologie*, vol. XXVII, 6, 1959.
2. J. Copans, *Critiques et politiques de l'anthropologie*. Paris : Maspero 1974; G. Leclerc, *Anthropologie et colonialisme*, Paris : Fayard, 1972.
3. In his study on precolonial Dahomey.
4. P. Clastres, Preface to M. Sahlins, *Age de Pierre, age d'abondance : L'économie des sociétés primitives*, Paris, 1976.
5. R. Firth, *Elements of Social Organization*, London, 1963, pp. 14-15.

SIX

Mohammed Mauroof

ISLAMICIST ANTHROPOLOGY
A Review of Some Contemporary Trends*

CONTEMPORARY changes in the world and the resulting discussion of new dimensions in the redefinition of anthropological tasks and purposes (as in Alagoa 1980, Asad 1973, Fahim 1977, Hsu 1979, Hymes 1972, Morauta 1979, Vidyarthi 1979 a and b) pose new challenges to anthropologists who seek acceptance amongst Muslim peoples and academic institutions. This paper attempts to bring into focus some of the key issues in this challenge by reviewing trends evident in the literature produced in common areas of scholarship in anthropology and Islamics. I will begin by considering a few contradictions and conflicts :

Conflict, Confusion and *Munāzara*

The identification of Christian ideologies, and evolutionary and anthropological theory, some of which is a reaction to Christianity, with one segment of humanity (Euro-Americans), and the corresponding identification of Muslims and Islam with another kind of notion of humankind and its evolution, pose

* It is my pleasure to express my thanks to : Professors Isma'il R. Al-Faruqi and Charles Frantz for their helpful encouragement ; to the NEH for a Summer Fellowship (1978), which made it possible for me to obtain some of the information included in this paper from the libraries of the University of Chicago ; to the Smithsonian Institution for a travel grant which made it possible for me to attend the Xth ICAES ; and to those Muslims, some of them students, who have sometimes wondered how I can be a Muslim and an anthropologist at the same time.

a besic contradiction. For example, anthropologists attempting to discover the origins and evolution of Islam and Islamic things (as in Aswad 1970, Diener and Robkin 1978, Wolf 1951) have found it unnecessary to deal with the Qur'anic definitions of Islam, or of the processes which Muslims might call evolutionary, which led to the delivery of the Islamic message. Any attempt to utilize such researches even for pedagogic purposes in Islamic milieux is likely to cause conflict and contradict basic presuppositions of Islamic belief and self-definition.

The contemporary growth of several developmental and progressivist ideologies based on diverse indigenous, national and international social psychologies in the modern Muslim world make the conflict appear even more vivid.[1] Within the context of this confusion, the philosophical and scientific task of unravelling the Islamic position on evolutionary and developmental questions has hardly begun. Anthropological research aimed at discovering the rationality of the traditional and contemporary Islamic explanation for the evolution of life forms, and of the development of socio-cultural entities, is much needed. If such discoveries are to be made outside the world of Muslims, while Muslims themselves remain silent and incapable of expressing themselves on the issues, the discoveries would have no relevance.

Anthropologists who also define themselves as Muslims can also address the task of answering the anthropological (and also Euro-American) critique of Muslims and the bases of their rationality. However, the definition of self and thus of role of the Muslim anthropologist, in so far as he accepts the humanity and rationality of the two contending claimants to his allegiance, is likely to be ridden with conflict. Such conflicts are inherent in the situations of change and emergence in which those who are Muslims have learned to be Western-trained anthropologists ; change and emergence are also characteristic of the situations in which they study, research, and teach as anthropologists.

The treatment of Ibn Khaldun and his genius by anthropological historians of ideas, when compared with the treatment of the same by Muslim historians, illustrates a part of the problem. Is a Muslim anthropologist educator to present Ibn

Khaldun to Muslim students of anthropology as he is to be found in Honigmann (1976) and Voget (1975), or as he is found in Enan (1941) and Mahdi (1971)? To Islamicist scholars, Ibn Khaldun's science has Islamic intellectual antecedents and consequences. He is an inheritor of an Islamic religious and philosophical tradition, dealing with questions arising from that tradition as well as of questions independent of it. In the much shorter incidental treatments of Ibn Khaldun by Honigman and Voget, however, that tradition is irrelevant.

As Muslims of the present age grapple with the conceptual and pragmatic issues of society, politics, and culture, they have to understand and deal with values that are the product of the religious and philosophical tradition that Ibn Khaldun addressed. The issue of revelation, the presumed nature of revealed knowledge and its relationship to thought and rational knowledge, as well as to the law and the community, were important issues to him as they are to Muslims today. They should also be important to those who wish to provide an intellectual leadership to Muslim peoples. But the most recent forms of anthropological knowledge, i.e., the end products of the histories presented by Honigmann, Voget, and others, show evidence of having relegated revealed knowledge to something akin to nonsense.

The rejection of revelation in the guise of modern anthropological knowledge has not been arrived at through the experience and examination of the forms it has taken in Muslim cultural contexts, but rather in Western lands. Hence there are no philosophical reasons for that rejection to be simply copied and imitated in Muslim educational situations. Rather, the reasons are political and practical. If one teaches Mahdi and Enan on Ibn Khaldun one is not likely to produce anthropologists, whereas using Honigmann and Voget may do so. Such anthropologists are likely to ignore the Islamic intellectual and scientific tradition which has a special relationship to Muslims. They are also likely to be despised by their community as agents of an alien way of thought, even if they continue to be needed. The paradoxes inherent in these compulsory kinds of choices among current contexts of scientific education and research in the non-Western world cannot be elaborated here, but it is necessary, to point them out.[2]

Muslim pedagogical needs, such as the one to produce an introduction to Ibn Khaldun that is both modern anthropological and Islamicist at the same time, is one of the levels at which the contradictions become apparent. Attempts to resolve may now be afoot. At another level, that of research the lack of an Islamicism to distinguish the universalist academic study of Islamic things from related but separate Islamic sectarian concerns may have had an effect.

The awareness of the cultural traditions and scholarship of Islamic polities unfortunately has been more an aspect of the scholarship of orientalists than of anthropologists in the West. Not only has this limited the attractiveness of anthropology to Muslim students and followers of Euro-American learning, but it has also stultified the development of the anthropological research of Muslim peoples, even within the limited range of the culture region demarcated as the Middle East and North Africa (Mena).

Thus, Fernea and Malarkey (1975 : 183), in reviewing the anthropology of this largely Muslim region, comment :

> . . .that, with few exceptions. Contributions to anthropological literature based on Middle Eastern research have failed to have an important impact upon theoretical concerns in the field of ethnology. Nor has there been an appreciable development of a fruitful dialogue between Mena anthropologists and Orientalists . . . In adition, anthropological studies from the Mena have largely failed to attract an audience of scholars beyond those devoted to undertaking such studies themselves . . .

As these reviewers see it the parochialism, and I might add aridity of Mena anthropology, derives from epistomological perspectives employed thus far. Their suggested alternative is not to correct the fundamental fault of previous paradigms, which did not recognize the need to formulate and employ epistomological perspectives derived from the peoples themselves, particularly from their own Islamic belief and value sets and from their own intellectual tradition.

The situation in regard to anthropological research in India, in brief comparison, is different. The anthropology of

India is a subject of engrossing interest to all anthropologists. Its development may be seen as a model for other non-Euro-American countries in their efforts to produce a modern behavioural science of human beings. While being a source of Western influence and part of Indian modernity, anthropology of India has also provided education to both Western and Indian anthropologists about Indic notions, values, and philosophical assumptions. Such ideas have become incorporated into the epistomological framework of the anthropology of India. Other than in the possible exception of the use of the paradigm of cyclical change derived from Ibn Khaldun in some studies of Arab society (e.g., Gellner 1969, Cole 1975), the anthropology of the Muslim Middle East and North Africa has been deficient in the consideration of explanatory ideas from the Qur'an and the Hadith literature, or from the philosophical scholarship of the premodern age of Islamic intellectual growth, in deriving models for the understanding of Muslim behaviour.

There are in the Muslim Middle East, however, a few indications of an intellectual response to, and feedback from, anthropological and historical studies of Islam done by Von Grunebaum (e.g., 1961, 1971). Von Grunebaum's initial attempts to develop a series of studies of Islamic civilization in anthropology, parallel to the study of Indic civilization initiated in the 1950s, have been much slower in germinating results than have the efforts of anthropologists who worked on India.

A step toward the fulfilment of that plan for Muslim anthropological studies is evident in the recent work of the Moroccan historian, Laroui (1967, 1976). The first of these studies has been by critics as employing a cultural anthropological methodology. The second is a detailed examination of Von Grunebaum's methodology and conclusions of his study of Islam. Von Grunebaum has thus reached the audience that other anthropologists, according to Fernea and Malarkey, have yet to reach.

Laroui's Arab and Islamicist response to Von Grunebaum's brand of anthropology is, notably, also an expression of an avowed openness, an invitation to the anthropologist to concern himself with things Islamic :

> If we have no desire for the fragmentation of research to result in a cultural protectionism where each keeps his patrimony for himself and forbids others to touch it, we must submit to new rules of the *munāzara* (1976 : 45-46).

The *munāzara*, a term that translates as religious, debate is to Laroui the necessary dialectical controversy between orientalist, a label that fits Von Grunebaum as much as does anthropologist, and Muslim intellectuals. Other dialectical oppositions could apparently become part of the exchange. The new rules he establishes clearly are designed for greater communication, not only between Euro-American anthropologists and non-Euro-American scholars, but also between diverse types of scholars of the East and the West such as, for instance, between historians and anthropologists who are concerned with the study of Muslim peoples.

Other serious evidence of the germination of anthropological ideas in Islamicist hands is not easy to find. I was shocked to discover at the end of a systematic content analysis of articles published in several English-language Islamicist periodicals[3] that the overwhelming number of contemporary Muslim writers and journal editors are unaware of or ignore anthropology, although they are quite responsive to several other Euro-American scientific and humanistic disciplines. Their response to anthropology, which I labelled "rejection", shows that the anthropological education or Muslims (other than those who are anthropologists and publish for other anthropologists), has remained as woefully inadequate as the Islamic education of anthropologists who study Muslim societies.

While examining the Islamicist periodicals I did find a few articles, the central ideas of which may be derived from modern Western anthropology I attributed the presence of this element to the exposure that the authors have had to Western ideologies in general, within which several anthropological idea sets have become "normal". I labelled such responses as "appreciation" different from the "acceptance" that one may see in Laroui's work. Such responses seem to be rooted in the recognition of a kind of social and cultural anthropology in the multilingual literature of Islamic history. This literature, widely studied by Western orientalists, in the era of Euro-

American dominance in the world and more recently by Muslim Islamicists, contains a pre-modern kind of anthropology. The revival of interest in it is continuous. A few of the important ideas in such revival will be discussed subsequently in this paper.

Institutional Developments

The tendencies noted so far (with the exception of Laroui's work, which has been published in English and French) are somewhat psychological. More substantial are the developments of anthropological departments, curricula, research, training, and museums in Muslim countries. While noting that these developments have hardly attained an independent position in the public cultures of the regions in which they exist, comparable to their counterparts in the West, we cannot ignore their real and historical presence.

Notice of the historical development of Indonesian and Turkish anthropology, over a longer period of time than in all the other nations with largely Muslim populations, is available in Ellen (1976), Kansu (1946), Koentjaraningrat (1964, 1975), and Magnarella and Turkdogen (1976). In Indonesia, where the combination of anthropology with sociology has been suggested, and to a lesser extent in Turkey, where a separate tradition in physical anthropology has been noted, the emphases are in social and cultural anthropology. In Pakistan (see, e.g., Ahmad 1977) and pre-revolutionary Iran "anthropological" have also been "tribal" studies. In India, Ahmad has spearheaded a highly productive series of social organizational studies of the Muslim minority.

Archaeology has a well known and separate history in Pakistan, as in other Muslim lands. The development of that field separate from other anthropological endeavours may also be true of Sa'udi Arabia (Masry 1975).

These developments are post Euro-American anthropology events. Their institutionalization may appropriately be described as developing. These anthropologies are in a sense parts of, and not variants of Euro-American anthropologies. Thus a Turkish anthropologist need not necessarily differ from Euro-American anthropologists in his/her work even when dealing with Islam (see, e.g., Hanifi 1974). "Indigenous" is the non-European self-role identification that an Egyptian anthropologist has chosen recently (Fahim op. cit.), although that role definition may not always be clearly understood (Hale 1979). One important aspect of these emerging institutional developments for engendering variation is that many of the personnel involved are of Turkish, Indian, Egyptian Indonesian, or other nationalities.

The hitherto largely unpublished activities of groups such as the Sociology-Anthropology section of the Association of Muslim Social Scientists (multi-national membership, with offices in Indianapolis, USA) are, on the other hand, characterized by a closer proximity to the Islamic intellectual and philosophical tradition seen as a source of variant models for anthropological and *ummatistic* considerations. With or without Islamicist and *ummatistic* goals, regional cooperation among Muslim countries for the development of anthropology is a possibility for the future (*Current Anthropology* 19 : 210).

The further development and fruition of such educational institutions may depend in part on how effectively their educational leadership deals with the Qur'anic and post-Qur'anic Muslim scholarly approaches to anthropological questions. The study of such approaches and the consideration of their contemporary usefulness are crucial in some definitions of the mission of the modern Muslim social scientist (Al-Faruqi 1977, Al-Shaykh 1976). The argument needs to be considered regardless of whether one chooses to be a missionary or not.

A primary reason for anthropologists to examine Islamic thought is to see whether it can be applied in furthering our understanding of Muslim behaviour. But the place from which we exmine it is the vantage point reached during the past few centuries of the development of anthropological thought in a non-Islamic environment. The references to the Qur'an and Islamicist scholars—mainly of the past—in the following sections is not intended to suggest that their ideas and works are substitutes for present-day knowledge. Thus, the contemporary Muslim social scientist's.

> . . . Work must be free of *taqlid* or blind imitation, whether his sources be Islamic or Western. True, it is his duty to learn from the experience and thinking of the ancestors.

> But it is equally his duty to understand the Islamic spirit which moved them and observe loyalty to it, so that his work may be a recrystallization of it. As to the thinking and experience of non-Muslims, he must know it fully and benefit from it without hesitation or apology. The truth knows no discrimination as to source ... (Al-Shaykh op. cit. : 3).

If such a position is granted we may usefully compare modern anthropologies (for indeed we are confronted with many schools of thought, not one) with Islamicist thought and scholarship. Several themes pertaining to foci of interest are then seen to be common to both categories of knowledge.

Humanism

One such theme is humanism. The humanism of the early Islamic scholarly discussions[4] conceived of mankind in universal terms, as being contained in the known and knowable record of all human experience. Thus the historicism of early Muslims pertained to universal history, not only to the record of the achievements of the Islamic movement after the *hejira of* Muhammad, *Salla Allahu 'alaihi wasallam*. This interest in universal history, in part a product of Greek influence on Islamic thought, is also in part attributable to the definition of the human being in the Qur'an and other Islamic sources as being the end-product of a geneology that began with one original ancestral pair, Adam and Eve.[5] Furthermore, the Qur'an declared that all nations and peoples of the world had been blessed with the receipt of divine communications via messengers. However, some believed and others disobeyed (Qur'an x : 47, xvi : 36). The Qur'an also said, as Pickthall (1977) translates it :

> And of His Signs is the creation of the heavens and the earth, and *the difference of your languages and colours*, Lo ! herein indeed are portents for men of knowledge (xxx : 22).
>
> O Mankind ! Lo ! We have created you male and female, and have *made you nations and tribes that you may know one another. Lo ! the noblest of you, in the sight of Allah, is the best in conduct.* Lo ! Allah is knower, Aware (xlix : 13) [Emphases mine].

Islamic humanism was goaded by religion. Revealed knowledge, which created curiosity about all peoples, was apparently aided by the circumstances in which the followers of Muhammed found themselves during the first few centuries of the Islamic empire face-to-face with a variety of peoples, colours, languages with whom they had to contend for political and economic purposes.

As a result of such contacts there emerged a large number of *descriptive accounts* of the peoples encountered, including non-Muslim peoples. The fact that many of these descriptions in their original form were first-hand, factual, eye-witness accounts based on personal observation is worthy of note. Thus e.g., Ibn Batuta's *Travels* continues to be a source for the history of the regions he visited (see Gibb 1929 and 1950-1962), as well as the modern use of his and other Muslim scholarly travellers' accounts, e.g., by Davidson 1969, 1970). Al-Biruni's study of India, which partly on account of its advanced level of sophistication in method continues to be reissued in successive English language versions (Embree 1978, Sachau 1865), was another product of this ferment of intellectual activity. His concern with describing the philosophical foundations and mythology of Hindu behaviour, as well as the behaviour itself, presages the recent concern with problems in the description of "phenomenal" and "ideational" components (Goodenough 1964 : 11-12) of culture. His description even makes careful note of intra-societal variation, e.g. religious beliefs of the educated are contrasted with those of the uneducated (Sachau op. cit. I :27, 111), and that the caste system prevails even though some of the philosophers believed in the essential equality of all human beings (ibid. II : 137-138). Al-Biruni's tolerance toward Hinduism and the patience of his "natives" toward him stand in striking contrast to later developments in Hindu-Muslim conflicts in India. Studies such as these occasionally went beyond the recording of strange (and sometimes exaggerated) information on foreign peoples.[6]

We also encounter in Islamicist literature works such as Sa'id's (11th century/Hejira 5th century) comparison of the civilization of various nations. "He developed a general anthropology in which institutions are related to the various faculties of man," said (Mahdi op. cit. : 144). Ibn Khaldun's *Muqqadimah* is the high point of such investigative enterprises.

Looking back at that whole sequence of endeavours from a modern standpoint, it is easy to see at least one basic theoretical and methodological weakness. These studies, while being comparisons of human beings in general, and of believers and unbelievers, dealt with culture only in the sense of it being possessed by peoples and nations whom their authors considered to be civilized. Their main concern seems to have been with those whom they felt were the most evolved, ignoring the cultures of tribal and so-called uncivilized peoples. Their emphasis was on literacy and other "intellectual" achievements, instead of the total pattern of human behaviour, as the data from which "culture", could be inferred.

The emphasis on literature and literary taste reflects the fascination with "the word" transmitted in the written form, i.e., scripture. The absence of scripture or literacy among a people often led Islamicist thinkers to assume the absence of civility, and sometimes even humanity, among such people. The present-day anthropologist is keenly aware of the efficacy of oral transmission, and of the maintenance of culture among all peoples, including those that lack a scriptural tradition. He or she is thus likely to refute such assumptions of the old Islamicist scholars.

It is equally important to note that the supposition of these scholars seems to contradict at least two principles of Islamic faith :

(1) That all peoples had been sent divine messengers ; and
(2) That the scripture of the Muslims themselves was originally a spoken, rather than a written, Word.

The humanist ideas of the old Islamicist literature[7] are thus the result of humanistic studies. In modern anthropological sciences the humanist ethical principles are transformed into a set of rigorous methodological and analytical procedures consistent with certain broad theoretical goals. Thus we may speak of an anthropological tradition which has consistently pursued such goals over a period of almost two centuries in Europe and America. We can find resemblances in certain notions of early Islamicist scholarship to various ideas that have become prevalent in recent times.

However, the sources that we may draw on to make an outline of a proto-anthropological strand in early Islamic knowledge are primarily religious ; they are also from a section classified by Islamicists as *adab* literature ; or literary humanistic studies (Al-Faruqi op. cit., Von Grunebaum 1971 : 250-257). Studies pertaining to the descriptive, analytic, or comparative investigation of mankind have never been separate subjects in the Islamic curriculum. As such, the tradition of Islamicist anthropology is a non-tradition ; rather, it has derived from materials produced in the service of disciplines other than the study of mankind. Even Ibn Khaldun's effort to create such a science in the *Muqqaddimah* was done while he himself served as a professor of law and jurisprudence.[8]

The occasional references to past investigations of an archaeological nature for purposes of interpreting Qur'anic allusions to ancient events need to be considered (see Grunebaum 1961 : 50, 1971 : 25, 242, Hitti op. cit. : 386). At present, however, it is the relative lack of an archaeological angle in Qur'anic interpretation that is more apparent.[9] The poverty of the recent Islamicist study of universal history, required by the Qur'an (iii : 137, xxii : 44-46, and numerous other verses) is forcefully brought out in Al-Faruqi (1962).

His paper is a contemporary appeal sensitized by and reacting to a body of investigation and interpretation in West Asian history and pre-history, which are also crucial parts of modern anthropological knowledge. In making such an appeal Al-Faruqi has reopened the subject of universal history for Muslims. He envisages a pre-history of Islam, or a "Pre-*hejira* Islam;" i.e., a notion of Islamic and proto-Islamic communities prior to Muhammad, of a period of Islamic history that is unwritten and hence available mainly through archaeology. In such recent revivals of basic problems in Islamic studies (see Muftic op. cit.) there are again assumptions of a kind of universal Islamic "psychic unity of mankind," which is also a fundamental idea in modern anthropology.

Evolution

Reference has been made earlier in this paper to the Islamic concept of the evolution of the Qur'an. The Sacred Book certainly presents itself as the final authoritative collection of sayings pertaining to principles that were selected for the guidance of mankind over a long period of gradual evolution (Pickthall 1975 : v). But the proposition has remained an item of revealed knowledge (to Muslims) uncorroborated by studies of the behavioural, social, political, and cultural conditions of the different stages of the moral evolution proposed in it. As such, those who disbelieve in the Qur'an have ignored the claim.

Muslims themselves, however, have continued to believe in the idea of such an evolution, including the idea of gradual (in contrast to catastrophic) changes in nature. A concern with evolution as a category of thought is another theme common to Islamicist and anthropological literatures ; folk tradition[10] as well as literary works show evidence of this. Thus it is not surprising that Darwinian and post-Darwinian evolutionary notions in biology have found a responsive and sympathetic reception amongst Muslims (Bezirgan 1974, Khan 1976, 1977, Wadud 1971). The.path of discovery in the natural sciences and natural history, as well as the use of models derived from those sciences for the description and understanding of social and cultural phenomena, may provide a bridge between anthropological and Islamicist disciplines in the future.

Meanwhile, if the "world" in the idea of "World Anthropology" is not to become a euphemism for "areas of United States and European cultural dominance," i.e., if it is to become truly an international mode of discourse, Islamicist and other viewpoints will have to be heard. Discussions of such viewpoints may not lead to new scientific ; however, they can be very useful in the mutual understanding of divergent peoples of what we think of ourselves and others.

NOTES

1. Peacock (1978) comments briefly on the reaction of people associated with a contemporary Islamic movement to his anthropology.
2. The problem has its own class-conflict aspects. Bohannan and Glazer, (1973) reviewing the development of anthropology in Western countries, have suggested that it was, in part, a consequence of wider social changes, including the rise of the middle classes and their urbane, perhaps

humane, attitudes and philosophies. In contemporary situations of the developing world which define the rise of new classes, deep rifts between bourgeois mentalities, associated with the Western-educated, and other sectors of societies and their ideologies are not uncommon.

3. Back volumes of *Al-ittihad* (Indianapolis), *Islam and the Modern Age* (New Delhi), *Islamic Culture* (Hyderabad), *Islamic Review* (Working, England), and *Islamic Studies* (Lahore), published between 1950 and 1958 were scrutinized.
4. The volume of literature that needs to be covered for an exhaustive study is very large. These works in various languages are summarized in many studies of Islamic history recently available in English. Of the early Muslims who have contributed to the growth of social scientific thought, Ibn Khaldun has received a great deal of attention (Rosenthal 1958 III : 483-521). As noted before, his work has been commented on in histories of social and cultural anthropology. Harris (1968) mentions Al-Idrisi. However, the more exhaustive discussion of this line of academic activity in Mahdi (*op. cit.*) should be consulted. Von Grunebaum (1961 : 24, 34-36, 46, 50, 57, 71, 78 n.8, 81, 85-6, 123 n.16, 126 ; 1971 : 19, 20, 25, 34-36, 240-245) and Hitti (1970 : 244, 333, 382-92, 558, 566, 582, 609-10) are concerned with aspects relevant to anthropology. They both refer to the growing number of translations of the sources into European languages, as well as to Sarton's (1927-47) review. Only a small section of this fund of ideas is referred to here.
5. The ancient gnostic belief incorporated into Muslim folk-beliefs, as even among Sri Lankans, that the original man-Adam-landed in Sri Lanka (Ceylon) when he descended from heaven (and not, for instance, in Arabia) is worth noting. Both Ibn Khaldun and Ibn Batuta mention the prevalence of the belief in the central regions of the Islamic empire of their time.
6. Von Grunebaum's (1961 : 7, 8) inclusion of Muslims among those who made "little or no effort to comprehend the outsider whose status as infidel disqualified him as an object of dispassionate inquiry" in the "Middle Ages" is unfair and misleading.
7. Humanist ideas, as traced in the literatures here, do not imply that the societies which gave birth to them were also humanitarian in practice, or in social philosophies and policies. I am also not convinced of the Western argument that Islamic society was just as racist and caste-ist as other societies (see, e.g., Lewis 1971). The investigation of that problem is a separate issue.
8. To judge the non-tradition, on the basis of the criteria of modern anthropological science and its methodology, is hardly justified. Exact methodologies and unified theory continue to be goals and ideas, not facts, even today. As Soraya Noland, the Iranian delegate to this Symposium noted in regard to the old Persian texts, the lack of an explicitly stated method and theory can make it difficult to rearrange the old materials within a contemporary framework. But it is precisely

in attempts to do it that theoretical advancements can be made and a "tradition" discovered.

9. Pickthall's note on Iran (1977 : 710 n.2) and Muftic's (1971) view of Qur'an xix : 56, 57, xxi : 85 are exceptions. Both these issues were also discussed by Ibn Khaldun (Rosenthal op. cit. : vol. I, 25-28, and vol. II : 365).
10. The separation of the folk, traditional, revelational and scholarly levels at which evolutionary and other anthropological ideas are expressed by Muslims should be examined in a different paper. Thus, there are notions of "evolutionary" thought of *sufis* (Mauroof 1976 : 114-122). Shari'ati (1979) includes a consideration of evolutionary and other anthropological issues which combine folkloristic, Qur'an-exegetical, and contemporary revolutionary dialectical ideas

SUGGESTED READINGS

Ahmed, Akbar S., *Social and Economic Change in the Tribal Areas*, 1972-1976, Karachi : Oxford University Press, 1977.

AL-Faruqi Isma'il R., "Towards a Historiography of Pre-hijra Islam", *Islamic Studies* 1, 1962, 65-87.

——, "Islam and the Social Sciences", *Al-ittihad* 14 (1-2), 1977, 38-40.

Algoa, E.J., "On Indigenous Anthropology in Papua New Guinea", *Current Anthropology* 21, 1980, 251.

AL-Shaykh, H.E. Shaykh' Abdul Aziz Al., "Introduction, in Association of Muslim Social Scientists", *From Muslim to Islamic : Proceedings of the Fourth Annual Convention of the Association of Muslim Social Scientist*, 1976, 1-5.

Asad, Talal (ed.), *Anthropology and the Colonial Encounter*. London : Ithaca Press, 1973.

Aswad, Barbara C., "Social and Ecological Aspects in the Formation of Islam", in L.E. Sweet (ed.), *Peoples and Cultures of the Middle East*, vol. 1 : 52-73. Garden City, Natural History Press, 1970.

Bezirgan, N.A., "The Islamic World', in T.F. Glick, (ed.) *The Comparative Reception of Darwinism.* Austin : University of Texas Press, 1974, 375-387.

Bohannan, Paul, and Mark Glazer, "Introduction", in P.J. Bohannan and M. Glazer (eds.), *High Points in Anthropology*, xi-xix, New York : Knopf, 1973.

Cole, Donald P., *Nomads of the Nomads : The Al-Murrah Behouin of the Empty Quarter*. Chicago : Aldine, 1975.

Davidson, Basil, *A History of East and Central Africa to the Late Nineteenth Century*. Garden City, N.Y. : Doubleday, 1969.

——, *The Lost Cities of Africa*, revised edition. Boston : Little, Brown, 1970.

Diener, Paul, Eugene E. Robkin, "Ecology, Evolution, and the Search for Cultural Origins : The Question of Islamic Pig Prohibition" (with CA Comment) *Current Anthropology* 19, 1978, 493-540.

Ellen, R.F., "The Development of Anthropology and Colonial Policy in the Netherlands 1800-1960", *Journal of the History of the Behavioural Sciences* 12, 1976, 303-324.

Embree, Ainslie T., (ed.), *Alberuni's India*, abridged ed. (Translated by Edward C. Sachau). New York : W.W. Norton, 1978.

Enan, Mohammad Abdullah, *Ibn Khaldun : His Life and Work*. Lahore : Sh. Muhammad Ashraf, 1941.

Fahim, Hussein, "Foreign and Indigenous Anthropology : The Perspectives of an Egyptian Anthropologist", *Human Organization* 36, 1977, 80-86.

Fernea, Robert A., and James M. Malarkey, "Anthropology of the Middle East and North Africa : A Critical Assessment", *Annual Review of Anthropology* 4, 1975, 183-206.

Gellner, Ernest, *Saints of Atlas*, Chicago : University of Chicago Press, 1969.

Gibb, H.A.R. *Ibn Batuta : Travels in Asia and Africa 1325-1354*, London : George Routledge & Sons, 1927.

——, *The Travels of Ibn Batuta, AD 1325-1354*. 2 vols. (Translated, with revisions and notes from the Arabic text, edited by C. Defremery and B.R. Sanguinetti.) Cambridge : Cambridge University Press, 1958-62.

Goodenough, Ward H., "Introduction", in W.H. Goodenough, (ed.), *Explorations in Cultural Anthropology : Essays in Honour of Geourge P. Murdock*, New York : McGraw-Hill, 1964, 1-24.

Grunebaum, Gustave E. Von, *Islam : Essays in the Nature and Growth of a Cultural Tradition*, 2nd ed. London : Routledge and Kegan Paul, 1961.

——, *Medieval Islam : A Study in Cultural Orientation*, 2nd ed., Chicago : University of Chicago Press, 1971.

Hale, Sondra, A Challenge : "Indigenous" and "Foreign" Research, *Forum for Middle East Research in Anthropology* III (2), 1979, 7-8.

Hanifi, Jamil, *Islam and the Transformation of Culture*, New York : Asia, Publishing House, 1974.

Harris, Marvin, *The Rise of Anthropological Theory : A History of Theories of Culture*, New York : Thomas Y. Crowell, 1968.

Hitti, Philip K., *History of the Arabs*, 10th edition, London : Macmillan, 1970.

Honigmann, John J., *The Development of Anthropological Ideas*, Homewood, Ill. : Dorsey Press, 1976.

Hsu, Francis L.K., "The Cultural Problem of the Cultural Anthropologist". *American Anthropologist* 81, 1979, 517-532.

Hymes, Dell, (ed), *Reinventing Anthropology*, New York : Vintage Books, 1972.

Kansu, S.A., "The Place of Anthropology and Ethnology in Turkish

Universities, and Works and Studies Carried on in that Field", *Man* 56, 1946, 141-142.

Khan, Majid Ali, "Nature of Life in Biology and in Islam", *Islam and the Modern Age* 7 (2), 1976, 42-63.

——, "Science and Islam on the Origin of Life". *Islam and Modern Age* 8 (1), 1977, 63-85.

Koentjaraningrat, "Anthropology and Non-Euro-American Anthropologists : The Situation in Indonesia", in W.H. Goodenough, (ed.), *Explorations in Cultural Anthropology*. New York : McGraw-Hill, 1964, 293-308.

——, "Anthropology in Indonesia : A Bibliographical Riview". *Koninklijk Instituut voor Taal-Land en Volkenkunde, Bibliographical Series*, 8., Gravenhage : Nijhoff, 1975.

Laroui, Abdullah, *L'ideologie Arabe Contemporaine*. Paris : Maspero, 1967.

——, "The Arabs and Cultural Anthropology : Notes on the Method of Gustave Von Grunebaum", in *The Crisis of the Arab Intellectual : Traditionalism or Historicism*, 44-80. Berkeley : University of California Press, 1976.

Lewis, Bernard, *Race and Color in Islam*. New York : Harper and Row, 1971.

Magnarella, P.J. and Orhan Turkdogan, "The Development of Turkish Social Anthropology", *Current Anthropology* 17, 1976, 263-274.

Mahdi, Muhsin, *Idn Khaldun's Philosophy of History : A Study in the Philosophic Foundations of the Science of Culture*, Chicago : University of Chicago Press, 1971.

Masry, Abdullah H., "Introduction. In *An Introduction to Saudi Arabian Antiquities*. Kingdom of Saudi Arabia : Department of Antiquities and Museums, 1975, 13-16.

Mauroof, Mohammed, *The Culture and Experience of Luminous and Liminal Komunesam*. Philadelphia : Unpublished Ph.D. Dissertation, University of Pennsylvania, 1976.

Morauta, Louise, "Indigenous Anthropology in Papua New Guinea (with CA Comment). *Current Anthropology* 20, 1979, 561-576.

Muftic, Mahmud, The Prophet Idris of the Quran is the Same as Imhotep (3000 B.C.), the Builder of the Enormous Step Pyramid at Sakkara, Egypt. *Islamic Review and Arab Affairs* (Jan.) 1971, 16-19.

Peacok, James L., *Purifying the Faith : The Muhammadijah Movement in Indonesian Islam*. Menlo Park, California : Benjamin/Cummings 1978.

Pickthall, Mohammed M., *Holy Quran* [English translation]. Karachi : Dawood Foundation, 1975.

——, *The Meaning of the Glorious Qur'an : Text and Explanatory Translation*, Mecca Al-Mukarramah : Muslims World League-Rabita, 1977.

Rosenthal, Franz (trans.) *Ibn Khaldun : The Muqaddimah, An Introduction to History*, 3 vol., New York : Bollingen, 1958.

Sachau, Edward, *Alberuni's India,* (Reprinted 1964), Bombay : S. Chand & Co, 1865.

Sarton, G., *Introduction to the History of Science*, Vols. I and II, Baltimore : Williams and Wilkinson, 1927-47.

Shari'ati, Ali, *On the Sociology of Islam* (Translated by Hamid Algar). Berkeley : Mizan Press, 1979.

Vidyarthi, L.P., *Trends in World Anthropology.* Delhi : Concept Publishing Company, 1979a.

——, *Rise of World Anthropology : As Reflected Through the International Congresses 1934-1978.* Delhi : Concept Publishing Company, 1978b.

Voget, Fred W., *A History of Ethnology.* New York : Holt, Rinehart, and Winston, 1975.

Wadud, Sayed Abdul, *Phenomena of Nutare and the Quran.* Lahore : Sayed Khalid Wadud, 1971.

Wolf, Eric, "The Social Organization of Mecca and the Origins of Islam". *Southwestern Journal of Anthropology* 7, 1951, 101-24.

SEVEN

C. Scott Littleton

DUMEZIL *VERSUS* LEVI-STRAUSS
Some Theoretical Implications of the New Comparative Mythology*

AT FIRST GLANCE, the methodology developed by George Dumézil, founding father of what has come to be known as "the new comparative mythology" (Littleton 1973), might seem similar to that espoused by his fellow country-man, Claude Lévi-Strauss. Both scholars are concerned with the delineation of deep-seated organizational principles which are endlessly replicated in a wide variety of otherwise unrelated cultural contexts. And both have emphasized the extent to which these principles, or "functions," as Dumézil terms them, are non-reflexive, that is, unconsciously applied by the makers of myths, and so forth.

However, upon closer inspection it is clear that there are in fact some p-ofound differences between the two French scholars, not only in method but also, as Dumézil (1973 : 14) himself has recently suggested, in philosophical perspective. The purpose of this paper is to explore some of these differences and to understand why Dumézil has come to reject "structuralism" as it is currently practiced, at least by Lévi-Strauss and his cohorts.[1] In doing so, I shall, also have occasion to review some of Dumézil's major contributions to social theory in his own right.

The key to understanding Dumézil's philosophical perspective lies in his often repeated assertion that the tendency to conceive of social and super-natural phenomena in terms of

* I would like to thank Larry G. Peters and Udo Strutynski for their many helpful comments and suggestions on various drafts of this paper.

three hierarchical principles—sovereignty, force, and fertility[2] is, in the Old World, at least, unique to the ancient Indo-European speaking domain (e.g., Dumézil 1958*a*; see also Littleton 1973, 1974*a*: 152). It is not an expression of some universal feature of man's cognitive apparatus, but rather the product of the experience of a single, historically definable human community: that formed by the Proto-Indo-Europeans, who most likely lived in the steppes of what is now South Russia in the fourth millennium B.C. (Gimbutas 1970, 1979), and their earliest attested descendants, who eventually came to occupy most of the territory between Ireland and the Bay of Bengal (that is, the ancient Celts, Germans, Italians, Slavs, Greeks, Hittites, Iranians, Indians, and others. That other such genetically related communities have at other times and in other places—developed wholly dissimilar ideologies is axiomatic, as far as Dumézil is concerned. Indeed, given analogous historical circumstances, it is not impossible to suggest that a world-view similar to that of the ancient Indo-Europeans might have arisen independently elsewhere. In short, Dumézil is, in the best sense of the term, a relativist.

This, of course, as anyone familiar with Levi-Strauss can attest, is wholly different from the philosophical perspective of orthodox structuralism. Unlike Dumézil, Lévi-Strauss e.g., 1963, 1969, 1972, 1973) proceeds from the assumption that there is in fact a universal ideological structure, a "deep structure" characteristic of the human psyche *per se*, which is predicated upon the mediation of oppositions through what amounts to a neo-Hegelian dialectic (e.g., Lévi-Strauss 1963). It is a species-wide phenomenon manifested in the fundamental patterns of human thought.

Thus, as I see it, the two scholars in question are working at two very different levels of abstraction and inclusiveness. For Lévi-Strauss, the level is that of the human mind itself; for Dumézil, who is no way can be described as a dialectician, the level is the much more immediate one of a historically and spatially bounded set of genetically related traditions (Littleton 1973: 202-203; 1974b; see also Strutynski 1974: 42-47).

Yet despite this considerable difference in philosophical perspective, there are, as I said, some apparent methodological similarities between Dumézil and Lévi-Strauss. One reason is that both are to a large extent neo-Durkheimians—that is, each has drawn extensively albeit selectively upon the theories of Emil Durkheim and his school. And in the process each, in his own way, has made some important modifications therein.

Lévi-Strauss's exposure to Durkheimian sociology was early and direct. As Leach (1970 : ix) notes, his university studies included ". . . reading from works 'by the masters of the French School of Sociology'—presumably Saint Simon, Comte, Durkheim and Mauss."

For Dumézil, the road to a neo-Durkheimian (one must stress the word "neo" here) perspective lay through the thickets of nineteenth-century naturism, which he rejected out of hand, and the perils of *The Golden Bough*, which he also came to reject although not until he had exhausted its possibilities as a basis for a "new comparative mythology" (e.g., Dumézil 1924, 1919, 1935; Littleton 1973 : 43-55). By 1938, however, thanks in large measure to the influence of Marcel Granet and the discovery (confirmed by Benveniste) of a tripartite class structure analogous to the Indian caste system among the ancient Scyths and Iranians (Dumézil 1930 ; Benveniste 1932), he had come to the conclusion that the only viable theoretical basis upon which to rebuild comparative mythology was an adaptation of the fundamental Durkheimian idea that important social and cultural facts are "collectively represented" in the structure of supernatural belief systems (cf., Durkheim and Mauss 1903 and Durkheim 1915).

But the Durkheim proposition that society is necessarily anterior to religion posed some important problems. For one thing, although social tripartition (or bits and pieces thereof) was in fact detectable among the Western Indo-Europeans (e.g., the tripartite hierarchy of the *flāmines maiores* at Rome, the clear distinction between *carl* and *jarl* in Scandinavia, the Celtic Druids, etc. (cf., Dumézil 1966 : 147-157, 1958b; LeRoux 1961 ; De Vries 1961), it had already begun to dissipate by the time the several communities in question emerged into the light of history. Therefore, the one-way causal nexus postulated by Durkheim could not be supported by the whole range of Indo-European evidence, and Dumézil was eventually constrained to restate, as it were, the relationship between social and supernatural phenomena :

> . . . I recognized toward 1950 that the "tripartite ideology" was not necessarily accompanied, in the life of a society by a real tripartite division of that society according to the Indian mode ; on the contrary, I recognized that, wherever one can establish its presence, the tripartite ideology is nothing (or is no longer, or perhaps never was) but an ideal and, at the same time, a method of analysis, a method of interpreting the forces which assure the course of the world and lives of men (Dumézil 1971 : 15 ; translation mine).

The net effect of this recognition was a major modification of Durkheim ; social as well as supernatural phenomena (the content of myths, etc.) were but surface manifestations of a deep-seated set of "ideal" ideological principles, which provide a "method of analysis" and thus permit one to come to grips with the forces affecting human existence.

Levi-Strauss, too, has long since rejected the Durkheimian idea that social facts necessarily give rise to supernatural facts (Leach 1970 : 50) ; and, like Dumézil, he is primarily concerned with eliciting a deep-seated "method of analysis" which manifests itself equally in the structure of myths and social organization. But here their paths diverge, for as we have seen, Lévi-Strauss goes on to assert that a single set of structural principles is to be found throughout the length and breadth of the human domain.

In short, while both scholars have taken a long and important step beyond Durkheim, Dumezil, unlike his former colleague in the College de France, has stopped well short of any attempt to synthesize an all-encompassing model of the human thought process.

A second reason for the apparent similarities between Dumézil and Lévi-Strauss is that each has drawn heavily upon linguistics ond linguistic models. There are, however, some important differences between the types of linguistic models each has utilized. A trained philologist, Dumézil has made effective use of the theories and methods of post-Saussurian historical linguistics ; he has adapted the comparative method, with its attendant emphasis upon the evolution of genetically related linguistic communities, to the "structural" study of myths and epics; whereas Levi-Strauss was profoundly influenced by the a historical models developed by Trubetzkoy, Jakobson, et al., in which synchronic structural processes, such as the neutralization of contrasts, are emphasized to the exclusion of diachronic ones (see Leach 1970 : 21-12). Thus, while, Lévi-Strauss finds himself constrained to look for processes and contrast patterns that occur outside of time, as it were, one of Dumézil's principal contributions to general theory and method has been the demonstration that the genetic model need not be limited to purely linguistic phenomena, and that it can be applied fruitfully in the analysis of a great many extra-linguistic parallels—especially social and supernatural parallels—among communities sharing membership in a common language family.

Indeed, perhaps the most important single implication of Dumézil's research, at least from the standpoint of social anthropology, is that the language family is the primary historical and cultural unit. The search for a valid unit concept is as old as anthropology itself, and for the most part anthropologists have focused on discrete societies or cultures. On occasion, more inclusive albeit non-linguistic concepts such as "culture area" or "area co-tradition" have been advanced; and we frequently make reference to such generalized conceptions as "Western culture" or "the ancient Near East." But when it comes to systematic analysis, we have generally focused upon minimal rather than maximal units.

Yet if Dumézil's analysis of the ancient Indo-European tradition is correct—to be sure, he has not as yet attempted any extensive cross-familial comparisons—the inescapable implication is that all language families, at least at some point in their historical development, will be characterized by a common or genetically related ideological system analogous to (but by no means identical with) that evolved by the Proto-Indo-Europeans. For example, anyone familiar with the Uto-Aztecan speaking communities (e.g., Hopi, Paiutes, Aztecs, etc.) cannot help but be struck by the extent to which these communities were (and are) characterized by a quadripartite ideology predicated upon structural metaphors for fundamental spatial relationships, that is, the four cardinal directions (cf., Nicholson 1971). Gods, narrative episodes, colours, and even to some degree the delineation of social phenomena, are typically structured in terms of four-fold sequences. A good example is the fact that most major Aztec divinities had four aspects or "persons," each of which was associated with a given direction, colour, and so on (ibid., pp. 404-405).

Among the ancient Semites the replication of seven-fold paradigms, predicated initially, it would seem, upon metaphors for the five visible planets plus the sun and the moon, are equally striking, from the most ancient Babylonian literature to the old Testament. Indeed, the most widespread manifestation of the Semitic ideological system is the well-nigh universal seven-day week, which long ago superseded whatever indigenous Indo-European day-cycle that may have existed (cf. Strutynski 1975).

This last example underscores another significant element in Dumézil's approach. In concert with most contemporary non-structuralist anthropologists, he freely admits that diffusion plays an important part in the historical process, and that no community's ideology will ever be wholly determined by a single set of ideological principles, genetic or otherwise. Indeed, the Greeks and especially the Hittites lost most of their Indo-European heritage well before they reached the threshold of written history (cf., Dumézil 1958d: 91). In his recent works on Roman religion, Dumézil (1969-1970) has also emphasized the uniquely Roman features of that religion, which derive from the special character of the Roman experience, including the impact of the non-Indo-European speaking Etruscans.

The foregoing, however, raises yet another important implication. If Dumézil is correct, no matter how great the differences in size, level of technology, or degree of overall cultural elaboration among communities speaking genetically related languages, if no other ideology has intruded itself to the degree that it has totally obliterated all earlier habits of thought—a condition rarely if ever encountered—there will remain a common core of ideological similarity. Even Greece, despite the extent to which it was indebted to the non-Indo-European speaking communities of the Near East, presents some evidence of such an Indo-European core (e.g., Dumézil 1953); Yoshida 1964; Littleton 1970).

Thus, thanks in large measure to Dumézil's research, the

language family can no longer be conceived of merely as a collection of genetically related languages and dialects. To be sure, all language families exist in time and space, and there inevitably comes a time when internal diversification becomes so great that the genetic relationships can no longer be detected. However, in their carlier phases, say, during the first two or three millennia of their existence, language families clearly share a great many fundamental extra-linguistic cultural traits in common, not the least of them being common ideologies.

It should be emphasized that Dumézil is a social theorist *melgré lui*. Unlike Lévi-Strauss, he makes no claim whatsoever to have had an influence on contemporary social science (e.g., Dumézil 1973 : 14). Yet, in developing the "new comparative mythology", he has in fact made some fundamental contributions to general theory—contributions which, in their own way, are at least equal to, if not greater than those so far made by Lévi-Strauss. That an ever increasing number of scholars, especially English speaking social anthropologists like Rodney Needham and myself, have seen fit to follow his example, sometimes in the solution of research problems far removed from those upon which he himself has focused (e.g., Needham 1960a, 1960b), is eloquent testimony in support of this assessment.

NOTES

1. Dumézil has recently taken great pains to disavow any connections whatsoever, past or present, with the structuralist school. As he puts it, *Je ne suis pas, je n'ai pas à être, ou à n' être pas, structuraliste* (Dumézil 1973 : 14).
2. For a concise overview of the tripartite Indo-European ideology, see Littleton (1973 : 7-19).

SUGGESTED READINGS

Benveniste, Émile, "Les classes sociales dans la tradition avestique", *Journal Asiatique* 221, 1932, 117-134.

DeVries, Jan, *Keltische Religion.* (*Der Religionen der Menschheit*, Band 18) Stuttgart, 1961.

Dumézil, Georges, *Le festin d'immortalité : etude de mythologie comparée indo-européenne* (*Annalas du Musée Guimet*, Vol. 34) Paris, 1924.

Dumézil, Georges, *Le probléme des Centaures* : *étude de mythologie comparée indo-européenne* (*Annales du Musée Guimet*, vol. 41), Paris, 1929.

——, "La prehistoire indo-iranienne des castes", *Journal Asiatique* 216, 1930, 109-130.

——, *Fālmen-Brahman* (*Annales du Musée Guimet*, vol. 51), Paris, 1935.

——, "Les trois fonctions dans quelques traditions grecques", *Hommages a Lucien Febvre* 2, 1953, 25-32.

——, *L'ideologie tripartie des Indo-Européens* (*Collection Latomus* 17, 1958*a*, 429-446), Bruxelles.

——, "La *Rigspula* et la structure sociale indo-européenne", *Revue de l'histoire des religions* 154, 1958b, 1-19.

——, *La religion romaine archaique*. Paris : Payot, 1966.

——, *Idées romaines.* Paris : Gallimard, 1969.

——, *Archaic roman religion.* Chicago : University of Chicago Press, 1970.

——, *Mythe et épopée II*, Paris : Gallimard, 1971.

——, *Mythe et épopée III*, Paris : Gallimard, 1973.

Durkheim, Émile, *The Elementary Forms of the Religious Life*, London : Allen and Unwin, 1915.

Durkheim, Emile, and Marcel Mauss, "De quelques formes primitives de classification : contributions a l'étude des représentations collectives". *L'année sociologique* 6, 1903, 1-72.

Gimbutas, Marija, "Proto-Indo-European Culture. The Kurgan culture during the fifth, fourth, and third millennia B.C.", in *Indo-European and Indo-Europeans.* Edited by George Cardona, Henry M. Hoenigswald, and Alfred Senn, Philadelphia : University of Pennsylvania Press, 1970, pp. 155-198.

——, "The First Wave of Eurasian Steppe Pastoralists into Copper Age Europe. *The Journal of Indo-European Studies* 5, 1977, 277-338.

Leach, Edmund, *Claude Lévi-Strauss.* New York : Viking Press, 1970.

Le Roux, Françoise, *Les Druides.* Paris : Presses Universitaires de France, 1961.

Lévi-Strauss, Claude, *Structural Anthropology*, New York : Basic Books, 1963.

——, *The Raw and the Cooked* : *Introduction to a Science of Mythology*, vol. 1, New York : Harper and Row, 1969.

——, *From Honey to Ashes* : *Introduction to a Science of Mythology*, vol. II. New York : Harper and Row, 1972.

——, *Mythologiques III* : *l'homme nu.* Paris : Plon, 1973.

Littleton, C. Scott, "Some Possible Indo-European Themes in the *Iliad*". In *Myth and Law Among the Indo-Europeans.* Edited by Jaan Puhvel, Berkeley : University of California Press, 1970, pp. 229-246.

——, *The New Comparative Mythology* : *An Anthropological Assessment of the Theories of Georges Dumézil.* Berkeley : University of California Press, 1973.

——, *Je ne suis pas . . . structuraliste* : Some fundamental differences between Dumézil and Lévi-Strauss, *Journal of Asian Studies* 34, 1974*a*, 151-158.

Littleton C., Scott, Georges Dumézil and the Rebirth of the Genetic Model : An Anthropological Appreciation, in *Myth in Indo-European antiquity*. Edited by Gerald James Larson, C. Scott Littleton, and Jaan Puhvel, Berkeley : University of California Press, 1974b, pp. 169-180.

Needham, Rodney, "The left Hand of the Mugwe". *Africa* 30, 1960a, 30-33.

——, "A Structural Analysis of Amiol Society". *Brijdragen tot de taal-, land en volkenkunde* 116, 1960b, 81-108.

Nicholson, Henry B, "Religion in pre-Hispanic Central Mexico". In *Handbook of Middle American Indians*. Edited by Gordon F. Ekholm and Ignacio Bernal, vol. 10, Austin : University of Texas Press, 1971, pp. 395-446.

Strutynski, Udo, "History and Structure in Germanic Mythology : Some Thoughts on Einar Haugen's Critique of Dumézil", in *Myth in Indo-European antiquity*. Edited by Gerald James Larson, C. Scott Littleton, and Jaan Puhvel, Berkeley : University of California Press, 1974, pp. 29-50.

——, "Germanic Divinities in Weekday Names". *Journal of Indo-European Studies* 3, 1975, 363-384.

Yoshida, Atsuhiko, "La structure de l'illustration du bouclier d'Achille". *Revue belge de philologie et d'histoire* 42, 1964, 5-15

EIGHT

Ezra B.W. Zubrow

INTERNATIONAL TRENDS IN THEORETICAL ARCHAEOLOGY

SCHOOLS of thought seem to be a product of all academic activity. It would appear that they are being developed, accepted, and rejected at an increasingly rapid rate. This kaleidoscope of transient theories and ideas leave scientific observers slightly breathless, if not confused. In our own discipline, one hears such comments as "archaeology is moving in all directions at once" or "archaeological research has been fragmented by the theorists".

Yet, all disciplines are affected by a series of similar processes which define their history. These include the innovation process (the actual development of the new ideas), the ripple or diffusion process (the mechanism by which the ideas are spread), the echo effect (the development of revivals and the return to earlier ideas), and the derivation effect (the development of new schools of thought from the revivals). We shall be concerned with evaluating effects of the first two processes on a school of thought entitled the "New Archaeology."

The "New Archaeology" is similar to many other recent schools of thought, for it is the application of neo-behaviouralism and neo-positivism to archaeology. Its development has been made possible partially because the rise and spread of scientism to the traditional humanities and social sciences. It broadly corresponds to the quantification of sociology, experimentation in psychology, or the neo-Keynesian synthesis, as well as similar schools of thought in the other social sciences. For each discipline, these schools of thought have created a period of controversy, were partially incorporated into the main line of the discipline, and were partially rejected. For the "New Archaeology," this shift has been particularly rapid; it has been from revolution to incorporation in less than fifteen years.

Some of us believe that the explanation for the accelerating appearance and disappearance of such movements, whether it is structuralism or the "New Archaeology," ultimately rests not only with the idea but with the changing demographic and economic structure of the intellectual world. The last 25 years have seen a relative large scale growth in worldwide education. The growth of universities, teachers, and students has been particularly marked in North America and to a lesser extent in Europe. Figure 8.1 shows the number of students per 10,000 inhabitants, by continent, from 1960 to 1975.[1]

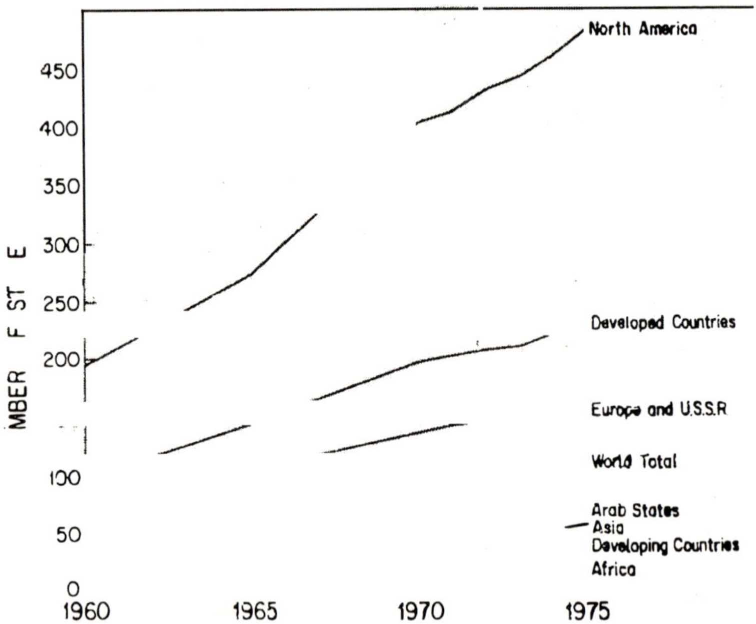

FIG. 8.1 : *Number of Students per 10,000 Inhabitants by time (1960-1975)*

The number of university students has increased over 21 million, while size of the faculty has only increased 1.5 million during this period (1960-1975). By 1975 there were more than 33 million students and 2.5 million faculty. Not only are the numbers of students and faculty increasing, but more importantly the students are gaining ground. Thus, if we examine worldwide data, we find that in 1960 there were 13.83 university students per professor; in 1965 and 1970, 14.00; and in 1974, 14.15. The worldwide averages mask some very large scale increases. For example, in Latin America for the same dates, we find the number of university students per professor increasing to 12.22.[2]

If professors are the primary producers of education and academic ideas, and students the primary consumers, the intellectual markets for ideas are becoming increasingly large, relative to the supply of ideas or producers. As a result, a new idea represented by an active *avant-garde* is so rapidly absorbed by the intellectual community that it scarcely has time to form and find a name—let alone be fully exploited; time must pass, new scholars must re-examine them, and they may once again become fashionable. Thus, there are cycles of revivals, neo-movements, and period of intellectual and cultural nostalgia.

What is the New Archaeology ? Historically, this movement appears to have begun primarily in the United States with W.W. Taylor's revolutionary *Study of Archaeology*. Examining the works of numerous archaeologists, he pointed out the discontinuity between their stated objectives and actual conclusions. Traditional archaeology was characterized as inductive, empirical, and particularistic. It ignored the questions of how and why, in order to concentrate on what, when, and where. It gave rise to a systematic study of time, space, and historicism, under which archaeologists still labour.

If Taylor pointed out archaeological inadequacy, Albert Spaulding set the stage by making change methodologically feasible. In a series of important studies, he showed new ways of collecting and analyzing data which made possible social interpretations. If one had the questions, Spaulding had the methodological tools for their solution. But, where were the questions ?

In the early 1960's, Lewis Binford in the U.S. and David Clarke in England began to ask about the role of archaeological theory, the role of archaeology in anthropology, and the theoretical nature of cultural evolution as seen by archaeological evidence. Both took a systems viewpoint. The former based it upon ecological theory, the latter upon information theory. Binford's students and colleagues, James Deetz, Bill Longacre, John Fritz, and Fred Plog, to name a few, began applying and field-testing his ideas. Simultaneously in England, David Clarke's ideas were similarly popular with the young English archaeologists, such as Colin Renfrew, Norman Hammond, and Ian Hodder. From there it spread until it was widely recognized and discussed, if not actually used.

In 1972, I attempted to estimate the importance and developmental status of the "New Archaeology" (Zubrow, 1972). I followed Kuhn in claiming that disciplines go through stages of development. These stages were labelled preparadigmatic (when numerous schools of thought contend for prominence), paradigmatic (when there exists a generally accepted set of grounded theories), normally scientific (when the theories are logically explored, tested and fleshed out), and dialectic (when sufficiently anomalies are shown in the result of the normal science that new theories attack the previous paradigm). I attempted to evaluate where on this scale the "New Archaeology" was located. My methodology was to use a citation analysis. I chose 80 well-known scholars who had articles or books on the archaeological aspects of environment, subsistence, and society published between 1968 and 1972. I collected all the citations they used to develop a bibliographic sample of 2092 references by over 800 authors.

I claimed that articles have differing lives; some are short lived, being seldom cited or even read after publication, whereas others have long lives and are continually cited. For example, classical works are light citors, but heavily cited, while review articles are heavy citors, and lightly cited. Reviews are seldom classics and have only short lives, for new times bring new innovations and literature and reviews become obsolete. Indeed, if a new paradigm or change in a discipline takes place, one would expect whole collections of literature to become obsolete, and new literature to replace it in being cited.

My initial expectations in 1972 were that the "New Archaeology" was a new paradigm. What should one expect to find in a citational distribution of literature if a new paradigm were developed ? First, a well-defined set of classic contributions that set forth the basis for understanding the domain of research with the framework of the new paradigm. Second, at least one well-defined temporal boundary. This "recency boundary" would correspond to the development of the new paradigm. There should be few citations prior to the date of the classic articles of the paradigm. Finally, there should be major differences in the categorical emphasis between the cited contributions published before and after the new paradigm.

What I found was surprising. In 1972, the single most cited reference was by Zeuner, a classic synthesis of Old World chronology, geology, and prehistory. It was followed by articles by Hole, Braidwood, and Helbeck, as well as by two new archaeologists, Binford and Flannery. No single reference made up more than .003 per cent of the total and all of the new archaeological references made up only .025 per cent of the population. I concluded that although I could demonstrate a recency barrier, there really were no new classics. There was not any significant changes in categorical distribution of types and topics and authors. Thus, I concluded that we were probably at the pre-paradigmatic stage. Indeed, the authors most frequently cited came from a variety of positions. In 1972, there did not appear to be a Keynes or Samuelson of archaeology—at least in print.

For this paper I wish to examine three topics. First, had another five years made any significant different in the status of the "New Archaeology"? Second, did acceptance of the "New Archaeology" depend upon geographic location? Third, where does archaeology appear to be moving in the 1980's? In order to answer the first question, I began by examining the *Social Science Citation Index* for 1977 and 1978. The most cited "New Archaeologists" out of a list of 35 were W.W. Taylor, David Clarke, James Hill, Kent Flannery, and Lewis Binford, ranging from 98 to 565 citations, respectively. Since David Clarke was generally acknowledged as the leading English theorist and Lewis Binford as the leading American theorist in the "New Archaeology", I decided to trace their development through time, by examining the number of citations to their works since the origin of the *Social Science Citation Index*, (1970-1978). Thus, I created figures 8.2 and 8.3 respectively. Figure 8.2 is a standardized scattergram of citations to Binford, and Figure 8.3 is a scattergram to Clarke with standardized units.

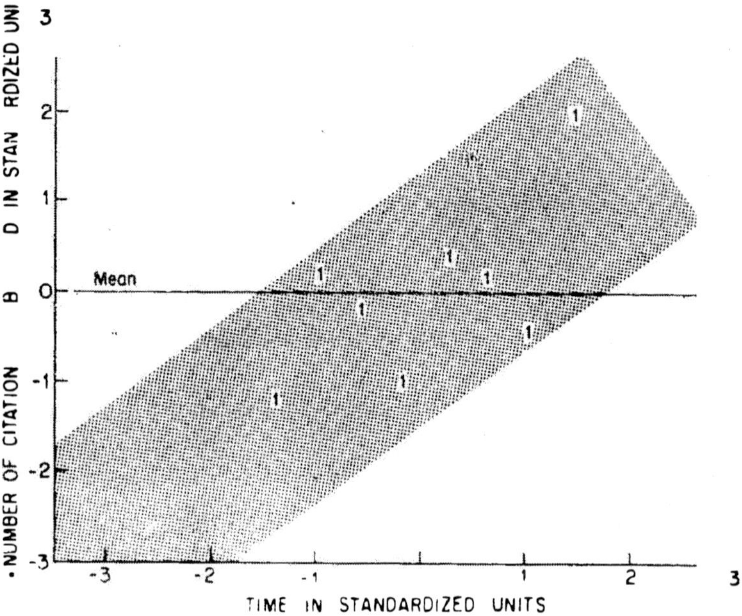

FIG. 8.2 *A Scatterplot of the Number of Citations to Binford by Time (1970-1977) Expressed in Standardized Units. The Data is from the "Social Science Citation Index". Vertical Variation : mean 46.4, std. dev. 15.5. Horizontal Variation : mean 73.5, std. dev. 2.4. Shading Reflects General Trend.*

Figure 8.4 plots Binford *V.* Clarke, and one may visually see the high degree of correlation; an increasing number of citations to their work, as well as the recency barrier, gives increased credence to the reality of the new paradigm.

Next, I undertook a survey similar to the 1972 analysis. The two samples were almost equivalent, with one significant methodological difference. The first sample was chosen from 80 archaeologists writing on environment, subsistence, and society. They used 2092 citations. The second sample was chosen to ensure contemporaneity and geographic variability. It consisted of 2984 citations based upon the work of 81 authors. It was formed by first systematically searching the *Guide to*

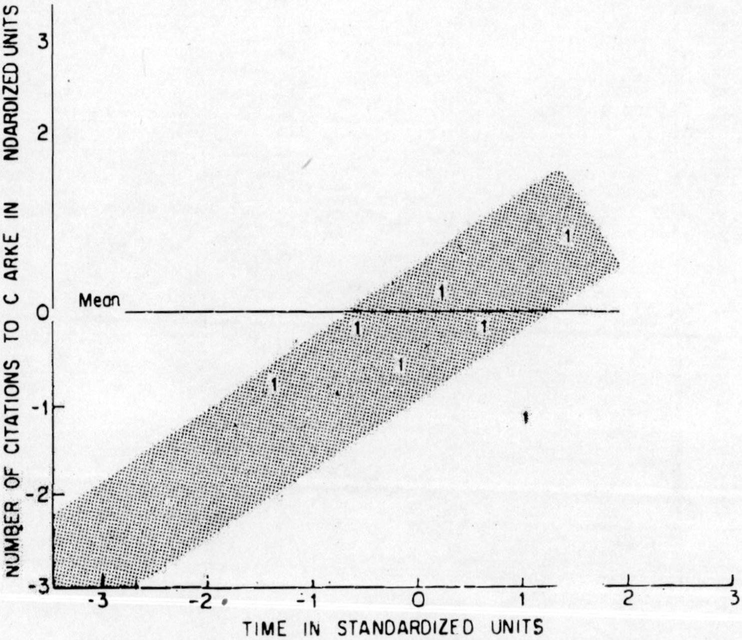

FIG. 8.3 : *A Scatterplot of the Number of Citations to Clarke by Time (1970-1977) Expressed in Standardized Units. The Data is from the "Social Science Citation Index". Vertical Variation : mean 20.5, std. dev. 3.9. Horizontal Variation : mean 73.5, std. dev. 2 4. Shading Reflects General Trend*

New Periodicals and Ulbrich's *Guide to Periodicals.* I then analyzed at least one article from the most current issue, 1976-1978, of every archaeological journal which exists in the 1.5 million volume library at my home university. (For an examplary list see Appendix 1) This represented journals from 27 countries, distributed across the inhabited continents.

The results of this contemporaneous survey were also surprising. Clarke's influence as measured by the number of citations to his work was approximately one-tenth of one per-cent. Binford's influence was marked by a larger proportion of the entire sample, at 7/10's of a one per cent. Clearly, one would not wish to conclude that they are individually central to the worldwide concerns of archaeology as expressed in print. But

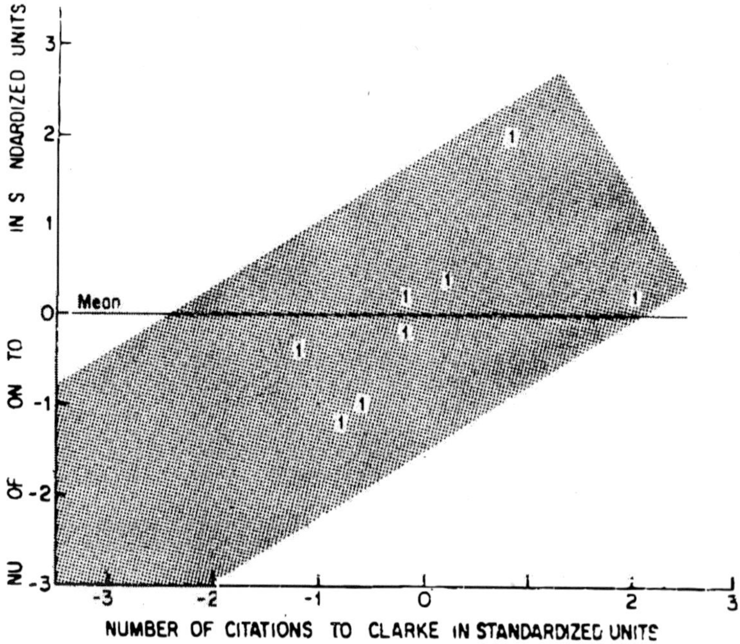

FIG. 8.4 : *A Scatterplot of the Number of Citations to Binford by the Number of Citations to Clarke Expressed in Standardized Units. The Data is from the "Social Science Citation Index". Vertical Variation : mean 46.4, std. dev. 15.6. Horizontal Variation : mean 20.5, std. dev. 3.9. Shading Reflects General Trend*

as a group there is a significant increase in the number of citations that refer to the works of the new archaeology. In the contemporaneous survey they represent some 208 references, or seven per cent of the total. This is enough to define a central theme.

Perhaps, what is even more indicative of the change in archaeology is encapsulated by a single article. It was not only the contents, but also the writer and the journal which were symbolically important. In 1977, Gordon Willey wrote "A Consideration of Archaeology" for *Daedalus* magazine (Willey, 1977). The "Dean of American Archaeology," the holder of the most prestigious chair of archaeology in the U.S.A., a famous professor at Harvard University, who is noted for his

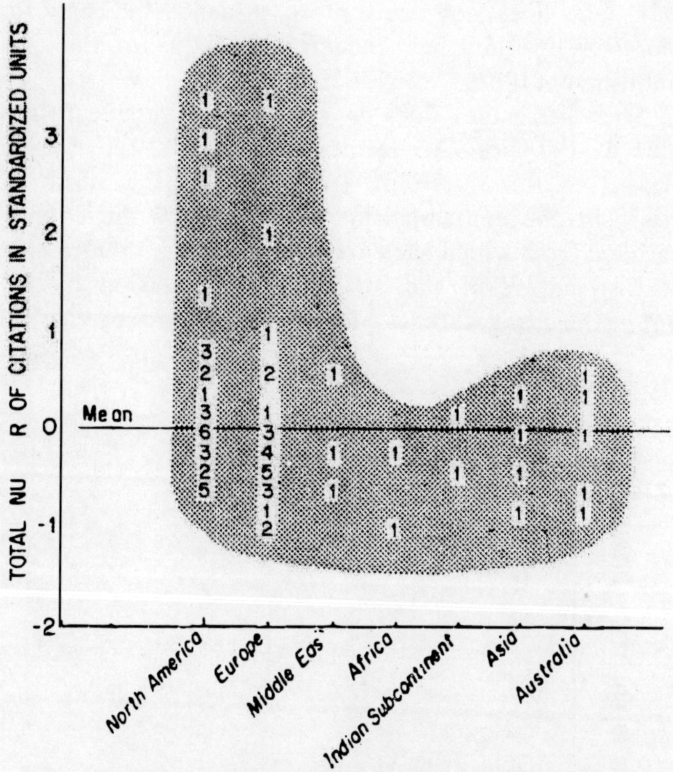

FIG. 8.5 : *A Scatterplot of the total Number of Citations by "Citor's Continent of Origin" Expressed in Standardized Units. Vertical Variation: mean 36.1, std. dev. 39.0. Horizontal Variation : mean : 2.2, std. dev. 1.8. The Data is from the Contemporaneous Survey. Shading shows General "Shoe Pattern"*

moderate, considered, and slightly conservative opinion, devoted almost the entire review article to the "New Theoretical Archaeology". Furthermore, he published it in a special issue of the prestigious journal of the American Academy of Arts and Sciences which is devoted to the reviewing the state of the humanities and social sciences. Noting history and problems, Willey concludes that it is not only a real, but positive change in archaeology, albeit an incomplete one. In short, it was a positive statement by the most important U.S. archaeologist in the journal most oriented to the national academic establishment. One does not need more evidence to know that this theoretical position has become acceptable to the academic establishment if not throughout the hinterlands.

The what extent does geographic location effect the acceptance of the New Archaeology? The next set of figures are relevant to this question. I characterized the author of each article in the contemporaneous survey by the country and continent from which each article originated. Figure 8.5 shows the distribution of the total number of citations by the continent of the citing authors. It shows that most of the citations

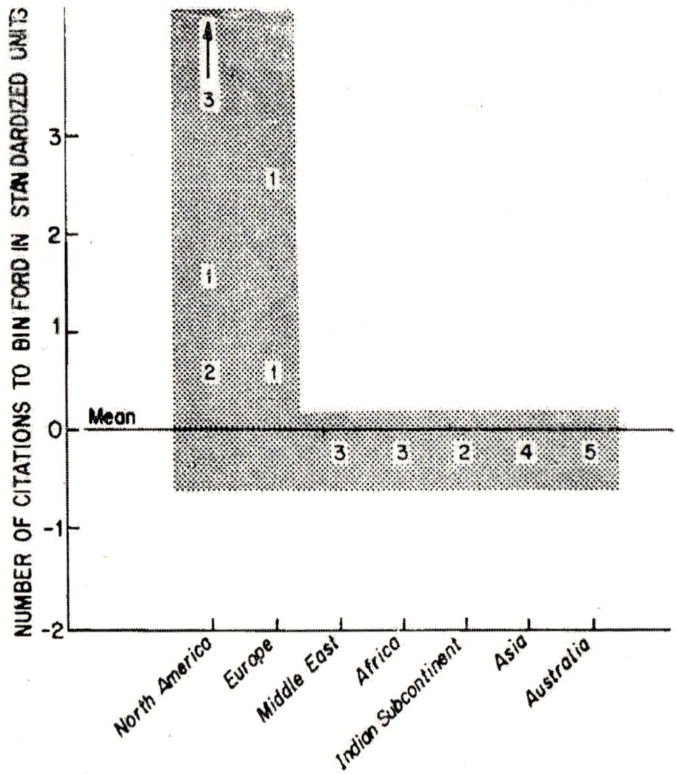

FIG. 8.6 : *A Scatterplot of the Number of Citations to Binford by "Citor's Continent of Origin" Expressed in Standardized Units. Vertical Variation : mean .5, std. dev. 1.0. Horiontal Variation : mean 2.2, std. dev. 1.8. The Data is from the Contemporaneous Survey. Shading shows General "L" Shaped Trand,*

were done by authors from North America and Europe. Examining authors, as one moves east and south, the number of citations begin to trail off. Clearly part of this is caused by sampling error, and simply reflects the inadequacy of the ordering policy of the library system. However, it is useful as a baseline against which to compare other works, thus for ease of reference, I shall term this pattern the "total pattern" or "shoe pattern". Figures 8.6 and 8.7 show the distribution of citations to Binford and Clarke, by continent. Somewhat surprisingly, both Binford and Clarke have both strong European

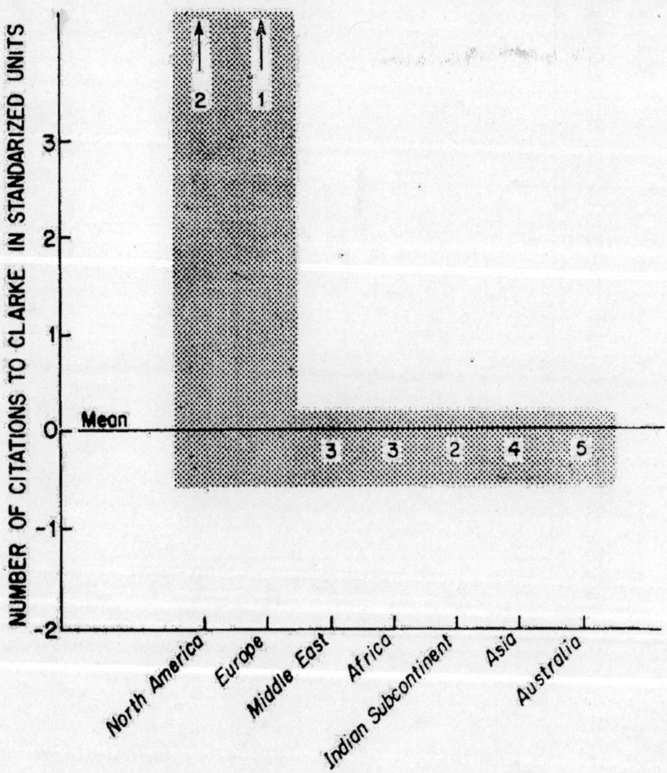

FIG. 8.7 : *A Scatterplot of the Number of Citations to Clarke by "Citor's Continent of Origin" expressed in Standardized Units. Vertical Variation : mean .04, std. dev. .2. Horizontal Variation : mean 2.2, std. dev. 1.8. The Data is from the Contemporaneous Survey. Shading shows General "L" Shaped Trend*

and North American followings. There is no clear pattern of North American preference for Binford or European preference for Clarke. However, as we shall see later, both belong to an exceptional group within the "New Archaeology".

In general, the clear dominance of North America and Europe are seen in previous figures. This dominance continues if one examines the citations of the other "New Archaeologists"

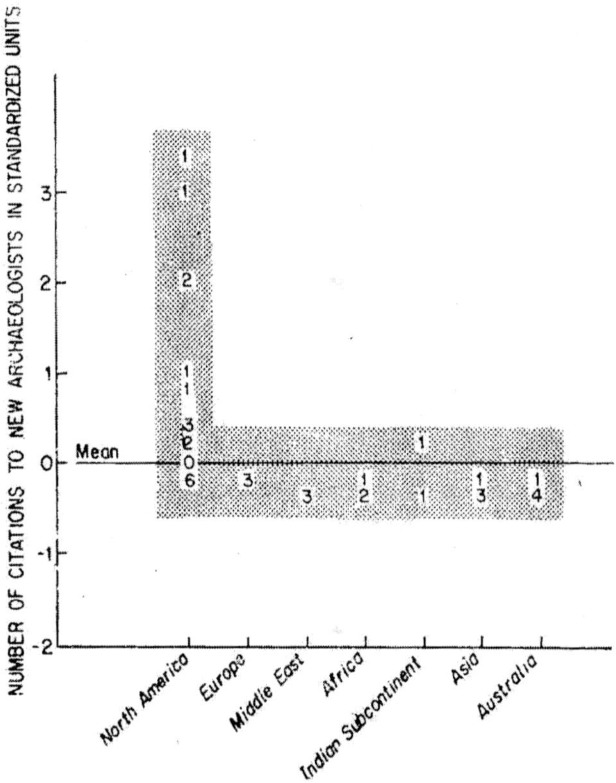

FIG. 8.8 : *A Scatterplot of the Number of Citations to "Other New Archaeologists" by "Citor's Continent of Origin" Expressed in Standardized Units. Vertical Variation : mean 2.2, std. dev. 7.1. Horizontal Variation : mean 2.2, std. dev. 1.8. The Data is from the Contemporaneous Survey. Shading Shows General "L" Shaped Trend.*

(Figure 8.8.) This sharp break in number of citations shown in Figures 8.6, 8.7 and 8.8, I shall call the new archaeological or "L" shaped pattern. It would appear that as one reaches the Middle East and moves east or south, that there is a true intellectual barrier or time lag for the "New Archaeology". It may be that the ideas are not relevant or that the time lags have been created by problems in publication circulation. Or, it may be new endogenous developments are taking place instead. Figure 8.9 shows the number of citations to traditional

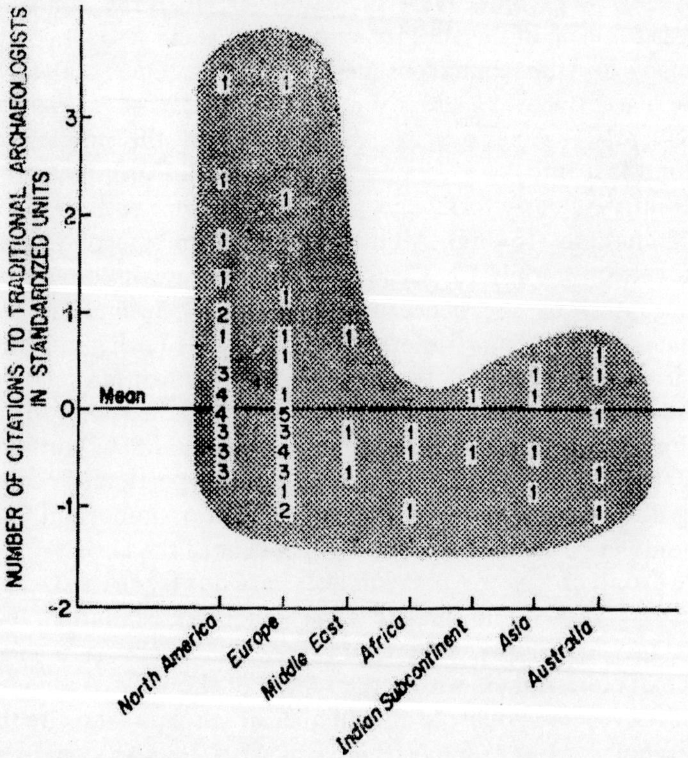

FIG. 8.9 : *A Scatterplot of Citations to Traditional Archaeologists by "Citor's Continent of Origin". Expressed in Standardized Units. Vertical Variation : mean 34.3, std. dev. 36.4. Horizontal Variation : mean 2.2, std. dev. 1.8. The Data is from the Contemporaneous Survey. Shading Shows General "Shoe Pattern".*

archaeologists by continent. It is clear that it follows the total or shoe pattern (Figure 8.5, rather than the new archaeological or "L" pattern (Figure 8.8).

In short, "Anthropological Archaeology", although widespread and becoming more widespread in North America and Europe, is not breaking out of these geographic boundaries.

I also did an analysis in the *Social Science Citation Index* for 1977 for names which figure somewhat prominently in the "New Archaeology." It is neither an exhaustive nor a necessarily representative list. However, it is the complete analysis for each of the authors, and thus in some sense is complimentary to the contemporaneous analysis. One analysis is across space, the other across time.

Several observations are relevant. First, the number of citations fall into two groups (Table 8.1) Binford, Flannery, and Renfrew clearly form a group of their own, with 55, 59, and 48 citations ($\overline{X}=54$). All of the others form a second group whose mean is only 15. Clearly, the former are in some sense more central to the concerns of the field. Second, if one examines the number of international citations (citing authors not from the U.S.A.), the citors of the European scholars Renfrew and Clarke are a far more cosmopolitan group (55 per cent and 56 per cent not from U.S.A.). Of the U.S.A. authors, Binford and Zubrow have the largest proportion of people citing them from outside the U.S.A. But more important than any individual pattern is that 30 per cent of the citors of this entire group of "New Archaeologists" are not from the U.S.A. Theory is clearly no longer a parochial interest limited to a single nation. Finally, one could conclude there is a high degree of cohesiveness within the school of thought. An index of cohesiveness would be the number of scholars who cite the same scholars. For example, there was more than 30 per cent chance that if the author cited one of the list of new archaeologists, he also cited Binford. Similar analysis with others showed similar results.

The third question, "Where is archaeology going in the 1980s?" is of course the most difficult. Several trends may be extrapolated from the previous discussion. There is no reason to believe that the increasing interest in theoretical issues will diminish. One may expect for another decade an increasing amount of interest in the "New Archaeology" and its practitioners as a group on a worldwide basis. In particular, emphasis will flourish in areas of the world where it has not previously been popular. It continues to be an area of interest to which scholars turn as the problems of chronology and taxonomy of the given area are resolved.

TABLE 8.1

Author	Number of Citors (i.e., Articles Listing Author)	Number of International Citors (i.e., not from U.S.A.)	Number of Citors who Cite both Author and Binford
Binford, L.R.	55	33	55
Clarke, D.L.	29	55	14
Deetz, J.	22	18	12
Flannery, K.	59	20	16
Ford, R.I.	6	0	0
Fritz, J.	9	22	5
Leone, M.	7	29	4
Longacre, W.A.	22	14	14
Plog, F.	13	8	3
Rathje, W.	12	8	2
Renfrew, C.,	48	56	6
Schiffer, M.	23	13	6
Taylor, W.W.	10	10	6
Zubrow, E.B.W.	13	30	2

In the same sense, there has not been a classic theoretical synthesis, perhaps because ultimately there has not been a body of cohesive theory. Rather, there appear to be a series of independent theoretical studies and methodological innovations which are approaching theoretical discoveries. One may hope for this synthesis in the next few years. Furthermore, it appears that a small group of contributors, rather than any single individual, have made the significant substantive studies in the "New Archaeology". This group is widening rapidly and should continue at an increasing rate.

If archaeology in the 1950s was historical, in the 1960s it became evolutionary. If in the 1970s it was processual, then archaeology in the 1980s will be operational. In both the 1960s and 1970s, major emphasis was placed on how cultures changed over time. Some scholars worried about cultures as wholes, whereas others about particular parts of culture, such as the subsistence or the settlement pattern. Key concepts were adaptation and how processes made possible changes through time. What was considered interesting was ultimately cultural change and evolution. How agriculture developed, and how it changed the settlement pattern, were questions asked in hundreds of ways on hundreds of examinations. In terms of systems analysis, people were interested in global change. However, as the 1970s have come to a close, the importance of ethnographic archaeology or ethno-archaeology has come to the fore, as people have tried to show the direct relationship between living societies and their material culture. The purpose is to show the limitations and strengths of the archaeological record. Similarly, experimental archaeology has become important. Real values are needed to replace old generalizations, such as that asserting peasant economies are more productive than hunting and gathering ones. Thus, people have been trying to find out the actual labour costs for hunting, construction, and agriculture. Both ethnographic and experimental archaeology have tended to emphasize non-global and non-revolutionary processes. Rather than worrying about how cultures change across time, they have begun to analyze the processes which allow them to operate.

For the archaeologist of the 1980's it will not be enough to show how the material culture changed, nor even how culture evolved and adapted. A whole new level of analysis will become possible—a comparison of operating processes across space and time, and may be even an evolutionary framework or scheme of operating processes.[3]

APPENDIX 1

JOURNALS EXAMINED FOR CONTEMPORANEOUS SURVEY

Acta Antiqua, vol. 23, nos. 1-2, 1975.
Acta Asiatica, vol. 31.
Aegyptus, vol. 56, nos. 1-4, 1976.
Africa, vol. 48. no 3, 1978.
African Quarterly, vol. 18, no. 1, July, 1978.
African Studies, vol. 37, no. 1, 1978.
African Studies Review, vol. 21, no. 2.
American Anthropologist, vol. 80, no. 3, Sept., 1978.
America Antiquity, vol. 23.
Anthropologica.
Anthropological Journal of Canada, vol. 15 no. 4, 1977.
Anthropological Quarterly.
Anthropologist, vol. 12 and 13, 1976, 1977, 1978.
Antiquaries Journal, vol. 57, Pt. 1, 1977.
Archaeologia, no. 122, Sept , 1978.
Archaeology and Physical Anthropology in Oceania, vol. 12, no. 3.
Archaeology in Montana, vol. 18, no. 2 and 3, 1977.
Archallogicke Rozhledy, vol. 30, no. 4, 1978.
Archaologischer Anzeiger, vol. 3, 1978.
Archeometry, vol. 20, no. 1, 1978.
Arctic Anthropology, vol. 15, no. 1, 1978.
Arkansas Archaeologist, vol. 16, 17, and 18.
Arxaiologikon Deltion, vol. 30, 1975.
Asia Asiatica, vol. 31.
Asian and African Studies, vol. 11, no. 1, 1976.
Atenea, no. 436, 1977.
Athens Annals of Archaeology, vol. 9, no. 2, 1976.
Biblical Archaeologist, vol. 41, no. 3, Sept., 1978.
Bulletin, no. 72, March, 1978.
Bulletin of American School of Oriental Research.
Bulletin of the Archaeological Society of Delaware, No. 11, 1978.
Bulletin Inah, no. 10, Dec., 1976.
Bulletin of the Massachusetts Archaeological Society, vol. 39, no. 2, Oct., 1978.
California Anthropological Journal, vol. 8, no. 1, Spring, 1978.
Canadian Review of Sociology and Anthropology, vol. 15, no. 1, 1978.
Central Asiatic Journal, vol. 22, no. 1, 2, 3, 4, 1978.
Central States Archaeology, vol. 25, no. 4, 1978.
Chinese Culture, A Quarterly Review, vol. 10. no. 2, 1978.
Chinese Sociology and Anthropology, vol. 10, no. 2, 1977-78.
Current Anthropology, vol. 19, no. 3, Sept., 1978.
Ethnographisch-Archäologische Zeitchrift, vol. 19, 1978.
I' Homme : Revue Française d'Anthropologie
Israel Exploration Journal, vol. 27, no. 4.

Journal of American Oriental Society, vol. 98, no. 1, 1978.
Journal of Anthropological Research, vol. 34, no. 1, 1978.
Journal of Archaeological Science, no. 5, 1978.
Journal of Field Archaeology, vol. 5, no. 1, 1978.
Journal of New World Archaelogy, vol. 2, no. 5, 1978.
Journal of the Polynesian Society, vol. 86, no. 3, 1977.
Journal of the Royal Asiatic Society of Great Britain and Ireland, vol. 10, no. 1, 1977.
Journal of the Siam Society, vol. 65, pt. 2.
Katunob, vol. 9, no. 4, 1977.
Kiva, vol. 43, nos. 3-4, 1978.
Man in the North-East, vol. 14, 1977.
Mankind, vol. 11, 1977.
Michigan Archaeologist, vol. 24, no. 2, 1978.
Mid-Continent Journal of Archaeology, vol. 3, no. 2.
Museum Helveticum, vol. 35, no. 2.
Na'pao.
New Zealand Archaeological Association Newsletter, vol. 2, no. 1, 1978.
Norwegian Archaeological Review, vol. 10, nos. 1-2, 1977.
Ohio Archaeologist, vol. 28, no. 3, Summer, 1970.
Pacific Coast Archaeological Society. Quarterly, vol. 14, no. 3, 1978.
Palestine Exploration Quarterly, vol. 19, 1978.
Pennsylvania Archaeologist, vol. 49, no. 3.
Plains Anthropologist, vol. 23, no. 81, 1978.
Quarterly Bulletin of the Archaeological Society of Virginia, vol. 32 no. 1.
Revue de Assyriologie et d'Archeologie Orientale.
Revue des Etudes Anciennes, vol. 77, 1975.
Reviews in Anthropology, vol. 15, no. 3, Summer, 1978.
Revista de Archivas Bibliotecas y Museos Madrid, vol. 81, no. 1, 1978.
Revista de Archaeologia Cristiana, vol. 54, nos. 1, 2.
Revista de Cultura Classica and Medioevale, vol. 17, no. 3, 1975.
Seria, vol. 54, 1977.
South African Archaeological Bull., vol. 32, no. 125, 1977.
Southwestern Lore, vol. 44, no. 3, 1978.
Soviet Anthropology and Archaeology, vol. 17, no. 1, 1978.
Tennessee Archaeologist, vol. 32, nos. 1, 2, 1976.
Western Canadian Journal of Anthropology, vol. 8, no. 1, 1978.
Wisconsin Archaeologist, vol., 59, no. 2, 1978.
World Archaeology, vol. 10, no. 1.

NOTES

1. UNESCO, *Statistical Yearbook*, 1976, p. 344, Figure 3.
2. UNESCO, *Statistical Yearbook*, 1976, Table 2.1. Estimated total enrollment and teachers by level of education, pp. 91-93.

3. This is not simply a matter of jargon. Allow me to briefly discuss a concrete example. Let us assume that one is an archaeologist and is interested in coastal trade. A historically oriented archaeologist would be interested in when and where the trade took place. A methodologically oriented archaeologist would be most concerned with how one differentiates trade items from other items independently invented and conceived. An evolutionary or economically oriented archaeologist would be interested in how it contributes to the subsistence base, and this base's contribution to change through time. An archaeologist whose interest is operational would be interested in what supply and demand values are necessary for trade to operate, what are the trade-off values for product switching, etc.

SUGGESTED READINGS

Willey, Gordon R., "A Consideration of Archaeology", *Daedalus*, 1977, pp. 81-95.

Zubrow, Ezra B.W., "Environment, Subsistence and Society : The Changing Archaeological Perspective". *Annual Review of Anthropology* 1, 1972, 179-206.

NINE

Profulla C. Sarker

ANTHROPOLOGICAL RESEARCH IN BANGLADESH
Past, Present and Future*

Introduction

IN THIS paper an attempt has been made to explore, in some detail, a fairly wide range of studies of anthropology. It deals with published and unpublished studies and research currently under way. It also indicates some areas which are believed to be important for future studies. It is not an exhaustive paper. It covers most of the basic research works of social, political economic, tribal and population anthropology in a broad sense. In this paper the nature of the study has been divided in different specific aspects which coincide more or less with the field of anthropology. Besides, this paper may help us to know about the problems and prospects of anthropological research in Bangladesh faced specifically by the younger generations. Different institutions dealing with anthropological research, teaching and funding have also been considered here.

The earliest works on anthropology are reports and notes

* This is a documentary research paper. The information of this paper have been taken from the original research works so far done and research currently underway by the social scientists specifically anthropologists in different times on various aspects of social, economic and political life in Bangladesh. The author is indebted to the researchers who contributed in the field of anthropological research in Bangladesh. Because their ideas and information helped him to develop this paper. He is grateful to Professor Clarence Maloney and his friends for helpful comments and suggestions made on the earlier drafts of the paper.

by administrators, missionaries, and travellers who contributed interesting information on the customs and the way of life of the people of Bengal. Also we have some secondary information consisting mainly of castes and tribes based upon scanty, patchy, general and qualitative information provided by teachers, clerks, and the officers of the British administration in connection with various census operations. During the British period we also find somewhat serious attempts to portray the tribal cultures by authors (i.e., administrators, missionaries, and others) who happened to be posted on duty in different parts of Bengal. Most of the contributions took the shape of long papers and personal notes. Portions of Dalton's book (1872) and Risely's volumes of Bengal (1891) are based upon such records (Kocher ; 1970 : 228). Besides these, O'Mally's (1916) *Bengal District Gazetteers* and Hunter's (1974) *Statistical Accounts of Bengal* provide both qualitative and quantitative information in relation to ethnological and anthropological research.

Unfortunately, in Bangladesh there is no scope for teaching anthropology except as a paper in the sociology course. In 1973 the Institute of Bangladesh Studies introduced the M. Phil. course in Social Anthropology with the help of foreign experts trained in anthropology. They are working here as Visiting Professors for supervising research works for a specific period of time. Some interested foreign agencies such as the Ford Foundation, UNESCO, US-AID, Agriculture Development Council (New York), etc. are also providing the lead in terms of financial grants and other incentives for anthropological research. Besides these, some leading social science research institutions of Bangladesh are conducting research using anthropological methods for data collection mainly, participant observation, genealogical study, interviews with key informants and in-depth interviews with particular informants and collection of their life histories regarding their subject. The names of these institutions are Institute of Bangladesh Studies (IBS) Rajshahi University, Bangladesh Institute of Development Studies (BIDS), Dacca, Bangladesh Rural Advancement Committee (BRAC), Dacca, Bangladesh Academy for Rural Development (BARD), Comilla, National Foundation for Human Resources Development Institute, Dacca and the

Department of Sociology of different universities in Bangladesh. Currently, a number of village studies are being conducted by Bangladesh researchers under the supervision and guidance of foreign and native experts for their degree-oriented research in the field of anthropology. A few researchers have already been completed their work under the guidance of foreign and native anthropologists some years ago. But the past records of anthropological research in Bangladesh have been found to be quite insignificant. That is why this paper is an attempt to cover and analyse systematically all these three phases—past, present and the future direction of anthropological research in different aspects of the life of the people of Bangladesh. Some of the indigenous agencies viz. University Grants Commission (UGC), Social Science Research Council, Integrated Rural Development Programme (IRDP) and Universities are also funding anthropological research in Bangladesh.

Social Anthropology

Perhaps there is no past record of social anthropological research in Bangladesh except Risely's (1891) volume on Bengal. However, in recent times anthropological researches are gaining importance to the academicians, planners and administrators. A few interested foreign and native scholars are working on different aspects of the social life of the people of rural Bangladesh. Recently, some of them have completed their research works. Jean Ellickson (1972) in her study *A Believer among Believers : The Religious Beliefs, Practices and Meanings in a Village in Bangladesh* (unpublished Ph. D. dissertation) describes the religious beliefs and practices of a predominantly Muslim village in eastern Bangladesh and the interaction between the religious and the social system. It also describes the symbolic system and the appropriate social relationships combined to produce in the minds of villagers the conception of living a 'good' Islamic life in an Islamic society. Profulla C. Sarker (1976) in his unpublished M. Phil dissertation, *Aspect of Caste and Social Structure in a Rural Community of Bangladesh* has analysed the caste and social structure of a multi-religious and multi-caste rural community in northern Bangladesh. This study covers the village economy, socio political organization, family size and kinship organization, religious rites and practices, occupational mobility, intercaste relations, Hindu-Muslim intergroup relations and Muslim inter and intra-group relations among the various sects and sub-sects. K.M. Ashraful Aziz (1976) in his unpublished M. Phil. dissertation *Kin Terminologies and Family Structures of Muslims and Hindus in Matlab Thana and Neighbourhood, Rural, Bangladesh* has made an analysis of certain cultural features which are shared by the Muslims and Hindus. Family size, social values, marriage and kinship are viewed as a set of role expectations ; role behaviour, role perceptions and quasi-kin terms have also been discussed by him.

Economic Anthropology

Very little work has been done in the field of economic anthropology in Bangladesh. R.K. Mukherjee's (1946) (published in 1971) *Six Villages of Bengal* is perhaps the first anthropological study on economic aspects in the northern part of the country. In this part six villages were selected for an intensive study of the life of the rural people with a particular bearing on their economic activities and institutions. The study provides a detail view of the economic structure of rural Bengal (present Bangladesh) offering thereby an instance of the socio-economic structure of Bengal in general. Profulla C. Sarker and S.K. Sengupta (1978) in their study *The Nature of Share-Cropping in Rural Bangladesh : A Case Study* are concerned with the causes and growth of share-cropping, patron-client relationship between share-cropper and share cropped institutionalized facilities and their implications in a multi-religious and multi-caste rural community in Bangladesh. An on-going research project in economic anthropology which will be completed in the near future is William Van Schendal's (1979). In his study *Peasant Mobility in Rural Bangladesh*, Van Schendal is concerned with village economy, specifically with the production system, cropping pattern, share-cropping, rural credit system and institutionalized facilities, for economic as well as rural development of Bangladesh.

Political Anthropology

Political scientists have published a number of studies on politics and political science. There is no previous record of research work on political anthropology or an anthropological study on political behaviour. Recently, a few anthropological studies on political behaviour in Bangladesh have been completed and some of the research works on political anthropology or anthropological studies on political behaviour are nearing completion. Peter J. Bertocci (1970) *Ellusive Villages: Social Structure and Community Organization in Rural East Pakistan* (unpublished Ph. D. dissertation) focused on distinction between 'atomistic' and factional conflict in which former takes place between two persons which does not generate any opposing group and later closes around one or more leaders. Bertocci urges that in the political context one's *reyai*, village, *samaj* and market area are political areas. A. K. M. Aminul Islam's (1974) *A Bangladesh Village : Conflict and Cohesion* is the first published anthropological study of political processes at the micro-level. He analysed how kinship roles extend ties to the neighbouring villages, and explained the role of 'brokers' who mediate between national and local politicians in bringing political change in the village. M.Q. Zaman (1977) in his unpublished M. Phil. dissertation *Social Conflict and Political Process in Rural Bangladesh* is concerned with the conflict and politics of a rural community in a village in the northern part of Bangladesh. This study indicates that the main source of conflict in rural Bangladesh is land and the villagers try to settle it at the village level through *bicar* and *salish.* He contends that village politics is basically based on faction leaders and kinship ties in manipulating and structuring politics at the local level. Van Beurden and Arens (1977) in their published research work *Jhagrapur* : *Peasant Classes in a Village of Bangladesh* present an analysis on land conflict in relation to rural social structure in a village in southern part of Bangladesh.

Besides these, some research works on political anthropology or anthropological study or political behaviour are on the way of completion. Nasim A. Hussain (1979) in her M. Phil. dissertation *Modernizing Politics and Changing Political Behaviour in a Bangladesh Village* analysis the process through which modernization shapes political attitudes and behaviours of the people in the village and measures the extent of political participation by the villagers. Shairul Mashreque (1979) in his M.Phil. dissertation *Kinship and Rural Power Structure : A Case Study of a Village in Bangladesh* makes an analysis about the political behaviour of the villagers on various issues—lineage, affinal and fiction in determining the power and the status of the leaders and the individuals.

Tribal Anthropology

A few anthropological studies on tribes of Bangladesh have been published by foreign scholars in different times. But unfortunately there is no record of anthropological study on tribal people which has been completed by native scholars excepting Abdus Sattar's (1971) work. At present two Bangladesh scholars are working on tribal people specifically on Paharia of Rajshahi and Khasi of Sylhet district. E.T.Dalton (1872) in his study *Descriptive Ethnology of Bengal* covered the selected tribes and castes of Bengal (now Bengladesh). Their social and political organization, religion and belief system, tribal life and institutions. It also describes the tribal customs and theories regarding their origin and racial affiliation. Lucien Bernot (1958) in his study *Tribes of the Chittagong Hill Tracts* has presented a description about the Marma, Chakma, Tanchingya, Banjogi, Sak, Mrong, Mro, Khyang, Pankho and Khami tribe and their economic life, social organization and customs. This book is the first monograph on tribal anthropology of Bangladesh, published by Asiatic Society of Pakistan. Pierre Bessaignet (1960) in his study *Tribes of the Northern Border of East Pakistan* is concerned about the general picture of the tribes of six districts of East Pakistan, Rajshahi, Bogra, Rangpur, and Dinajpur on the one hand; and Mymensingh and Sylhet on the other. This study has made a sharp distinction between these two groups because of their separate origins : the tribes of the four western districts are of "Mundo-Dravidian Stock" and come from Chota Nagpur and the Santhal Parganas, while those of the later two districts are 'Mongoloid' and come from the Assam Hills. Abdus Sattar (1971) in his book *In the Sylvan Shadows* deals with the aboriginal tribes of Bangladesh. This study focuses on primitive way of life, peculiar tribal organization in society hardened by age-long customs, tradition, rituals and religious beliefs, separate ethnological entity and comparative inpregnability of tractless hills and ever green forest of the region all have combined to invest it with an excessiveness uncommon in other parts of the country.

Now, we shall discuss about the on-going research project of tribal anthropology which are expected to be completed in future. Fr. Stephen G. Gomes (1979) in his study *Social Organization of the Paharias : A Village Study of A Tribal Community in Bangladesh* is concerned about the origin of Paharias, their family and kinship pattern, different phases of their life—birth, marriage, and death, their economic and political organization and their way of life in changing Bengladesh today. S. Mortuza Hasan (1970) in his study *Khasis is Bangladesh : Problems of a Peripheral Tribal Community* is concerned about the Khasis with special focus on the leadership and politics, description of Khasis political system with the view of analyzing how it fits with the wider political system and what administrative adjustments are required.

Population Anthropology

Population is one of the main national problems of Bangladesh. If the existing rate of population growth is not checked then the fruits of our economic and social development may end in smoke. Many social scientists, especially sociologists, social workers, economists, statisticians, demographers and geographers have done a lot of research works in the field of population and family planning through survey method. But no single research work has been done by the anthropologists on population in Bangladesh. Recently, Clarence T. Maloney, Profulla C. Sarker, Ashraful Aziz (1977) have taken a research project on population entitled "World View and Belief System in Relation to Population in Bangladesh". The project is conducted by the Institute of Bangladesh Studies, Rajshahi University and is financed by the US-AID. The entire research report is expected to be published by the Oxford University Press, Dacca in 1979. The main theme of the research project is to indicate one's perception of the world about him, its teleology, and the powers and causes affecting one's environment, crops, animals, family, health, and reproduction. Belief system implies all active beliefs, both those organized as formal systems with ideologies and rituals and those beliefs and ideas stemming from older levels of culture not organized in over-reaching religious system. Its crucial aspect is the said beliefs and philosophical views which in any way have or might have bearing on behaviour affecting population, especially fertility. Incidentally it is the first research project on population anthropology in Bangladesh.

Future Direction of Anthropological Research

Anthropology is no longer the study of tribal societies and cultures. Anthropologists, today, are as much concerned with modern societies and the civilization as are specialists in many of other social science disciplines. The theoretical and practical problems of modernization and development, population, national integration in new states, education, institution building etc. are of as such concern to anthropologists as they are to other social scientists. Very little works have been done in the field of anthropology, specifically social, political, economic, tribal and population anthropology in Bangladesh which are discussed elsewhere in this paper. Besides these, there are other important aspects of anthropological research which are very important in our country. Anthropological study of urban areas has so far been a neglected field. At present census reports and a few socio-economic surveys give us quantitative information about the towns, but descriptive accounts of a qualitative nature are few and lack precision and depth. Social Anthropological studies of towns will make a substantial contribution in this direction.

Similarly, very few research work has been done on agrarian social structure, medical anthropology, social demography, leadership, development anthropology, psychological anthropology, anthropology of social movement, athropology of food, anthropology of music, comparative study, etc. In future anthropological research should be done on the above mentioned fields. Besides these, in the area study programme, emphasis should be laid on the nature of inter-ethnic relationship obtaining among the ethnic groups living in the area and on the composite-structure and culture of the region.

Physical anthropological research is quite absent in Bangladesh. Physical anthropology deals with man as a biological animal : his origins and sub-human relations; early man, and development of modern man, with stress upon racial and other differentiation. Anthropologists can devote considerable attention to the problem of relating the biological characteristics of man to his cultural activities. In Bangladesh emphasis should be given on physical anthropological research which will promote human understanding and racial integration in future.

Prospects and Problems of Anthropological Research

It is evident from the foregoing discussion that there exists a bright and virgin field of anthropology in Bangladesh. People of different religious groups, tribes, cultures, and sub-cultures are residing in Bangladesh. Anthropological research is essential to know these people and their way of life, language, economy, politics, social structure, kinship organization, family, customs, rituals, beliefs, food habits, group conflicts, intergroup relations, their various types of problems and so on. I may mention here that enough statistical information are not available in Bangladesh. People hesitate to divulge facts about their way of life due to illiteracy and shyness. Therefore, participant observation is perhaps the only way to collect the information effectively. Hence, an initiative should be taken by the Government and the universities to open up research facilities and academic department to train and to produce anthropologists in future.

Anthropological research in Bangladesh is confronted with the following problems :

(a) Lack of trained personnel in the field of anthropology,

(b) Lack of anthropological institutions (e.g., anthropological survey of Bangladesh),

(c) Administrators and planners have not yet been able to appreciate the importance of anthropological studies,

(d) Difficulties in having access to official records and documents,

(e) Lack of adequate funds for anthropological research,

(f) Problems of field work :

(i) Problem of contacting the respondent. This becomes an acute problem for the field worker in conducting their field work in the rural areas, especially in the rainy season. During this period the field worker can move neither by boat nor on food and faces the problem of conducting field work,

(ii) Misunderstanding; most of the time the field investigator is confused as government employee,

(iii) Interference by others; it is observed that when any field worker approaches any respondent, some of the neighbours, village leaders, or relations of the respondent appears there and tries to answer questions on behalf of the respondent. Under such circumstances exact data can hardly be collected,

(iv) Avoiding tendency of the respondent; majority of our people are illiterate and quite ignorant of the importance of social research. They try to avoid interview as far as possible,

(v) Unnecessary fear; experience shows that most of our people are afraid of interview. They think that the interview may bring some unforeseen danger for them like imposition of more tax,

(vi) Inability to express; this is a problem because most of our people are illiterate especially in rural areas who sometimes know the facts but cannot express,

(vii) Materialistic attitude; due to pressure of poverty our people try to get some material benefit from their work. If they are given to understand that research will bring no material benefit for them, they show no response to it or they feel uneasy to express,

(viii) Superstitions and conservativeness; majority of our people, especially rural people, are superstitious and conservative in nature.

Due to this conservativeness they do not like to disclose their private affairs to others. This was become a serious handicap to research especially in the field of family planning. This problem is more acute if the field worker is a male and the respondent is female one.

Conclusion

In conclusion it can be mentioned that unless the anthropological researchers are able to provide accurate information about all aspects of socio-economic and political complex, the planners and policy makers cannot be expected to formulate meaningful policies. At present Bangladesh is suffering from various types of problems, the anthropologists can act as social doctors in diagnosing the symptoms of social problems, and they may be of some help in the course of transformation of our traditional society. As mentioned earlier facts about different aspects of social life in Bangladesh are not well known. The anthropologists can be of much help in collecting information about the life and activities of the people in Bangladesh by applying participant-observation method. At present, large scale survey may not be helpful for collecting information in Bangladesh due to reasons mentioned elsewhere. Therefore, the govt. should come forward with all necessary help and support to promote anthropological research in Bangladesh. The young and energetic anthropologists should also be prepared to accept the heavy responsibility for the proper development of anthropology in Bangladesh.

SUGGESTED READINGS

Bertocci, Peter J., "Elusive Village : Social Structure and Community Organization in Rural East Pakistan", Unpublished Ph. D. dissertation. Michigan State University, 1970.

Bernot, Lucien, "Ethnic Groups of Chittagong Hill Tracts" in Pierre Bessaignet (ed.) *Social Research in East Pakistan. Asiatic Society*, Dacca, 1958.

Bessaignet, Pierre, "Tribes of the Northern Borders of East Pakistan", in Pierre Bessaignet (ed.) *Social Research in East Pakistan.* Asiatic Society, Dacca, 1960.

Ellickson, J., "A Believer Among Believers : The Religious Beliefs, Practices, and Meanings in a Village in Bangladesh". Unpublished Ph. D. Thesis, Department of Anthropology, Michigan State University, 1972.

Hunter, W.W., *A Statistical Account of Bengal*, D.K. Publishing House, Delhi, 1974.

Islam, A.K.M. Aminul, *A Bangladesh Village : Conflict and Cohesion*, Sehenkman Publishing Company, Cambridge, 1974.

Mukherjee, R.K., *Six Villages of Bengal*. Popular Prakashan, Bombay, 1971.

Nicholas, Ralph W., "Some Uses for Social Anthropology in Bangladesh". The Ford Foundation, Dacca, 1973.

O'Mally, L.S.S., Bengal District Gazetteers. Bengal Secretariat Book Depot, Calcutta, 1916.

Satter, Abdus, *In the Sylvan Shadows*, Saquib Brothers, Dacca, 1971.

Sraker, Profulla C. "Aspect of Caste and Social Structure in a Village of Bangladesh". An unpublished M. Phil. Thesis, Institute of Bangladesh Studies, Rajshahi University, 1976.

TEN

Profulla C. Sarker

MUSLIM INTERGROUP RELATIONS AND THE PROCESS OF DEVELOPMENT IN RURAL BANGLADESH*

Introduction

ISLAM FORMALLY does not approve of social discrimination between men in terms of wealth, birth, and colour. Islam also recognizes the equality, brotherhood, and fraternity of all Muslims. But social differentiation can be found among the Muslims in terms of their affiliation of different *mojhāb* (Islam; 1974 : 83). Sometime after the death of Prophet Mohammad, the Muslim community divided into two major divisions—Shi'a and Sunni. The Shi'as are the followers of Ali, first cousin of Mohammad and the husband of his daughter Fatima. The Shi'as maintain that Ali was the first legitimate Imam or *Khālifāh* or successor to the Prophet, and therefore, they refuse to recognise Abu Bakar, Omar and Osman as *Khālifāh*. The term Sunni is generally applied to the large group of Muslims who acknowledge the first four *Khalifās* to have been the

* This paper is a part of my thesis entitled *Aspect of Caste and Social Structure in a Rural Community of Bangladesh* for the degree of M. Phil. in Social Anthropology. I have spent twelve months doing field work in Mohānandākhāli. An initial stay of ten months in 1975-76. A second visit of two months in 1977 for the pilot survey of a project named *World View and Belief System in Relation to Population in Bangladesh*. I am grateful to Professor Safiuddin Joarder, Professor J. Kirkpatrick, Professor Clarence T. Maloney and Professor A.K.M. Aminul Islam for advice and guidance. I am also indebted to the Institute of Bangladesh Studies and US-AID for financing the project.

rightful successors of Mohammad, and who belong to one of the four schools of jurisprudence founded by Imam Abu Hanifa. Imam ash-Shahi, Imam Ahmed ibn Hambal and Imam Malik.

In Mahānandākhāli all Muslims belong to the Sūnni division. The Sūnni division is divided again into four *mojhābs*, the first three of which are the Hanafi, Shafi and Hambali. The fourth mojhāb, Maliki, the followers of Imam Malik. But Malikis are very rare in Bangladesh. Besides these, there is another group of Muslims who do not recognise any of the four Imams and they continue to follow only Mohammad the Prophet is known as Mohāmmadi or *Āh-lehādith.* It is interesting to note that the Mohammadi division is called *lā-mojhāb* (out of mojhāb or no mojhāb) by the people of other mojhab, a pejorative connotation, as they think the Mohammadis are inferior to other mojhābs. It is my impression, as a matter of fact, that Mohammadis are minority group among the Muslim in Bangladesh villages, but generally speaking they and the Hanafis are the two most common mojhābs, and they contest for the honour of social superiority.

Intergroup Differences in Beliefs and Ritual

In Mohānandākhāli all Muslims belong to the Mohammadi and Hanafi mojhābs. Between the two sub-groups, Mohammadis are the largest in number and the Hanafis the smallest. The Mohammadis are 93 per cent Muslim households and the Hanafis are only 7 per cent in the village. But there are intergroup differences and relationships between the Mohammadis and Hanafis in connection with prayer, diet, marriage and divorce.[1]

In the village there is only one mosque exclusively for the people of Mohammadi mojhāb. The Hanafis have no mosque in the village. For *jummā-nāmāj* (weekly prayer) on Friday they go to a mosque at Noahata, a village nearly, where there is a separate mosque for Hanafis. At the time of namaj the people of the Hanafi mojhab pronounce the word *duāllin* after the end of the *āl-hāmdu-surā* (the first sura pronounced during namaj) and then they also pronounce the word *āmin* very softly so that nobody can hear. On the other hand, the people of the Mohammadi mojhāb say *juāllin* instead of duāllin, and they also pronounce the word *āmin* loudly so that everybody can hear. Now the question is, why should Hanafis and Mohammadis disagree on the pronunciation of one word? The Mohammadis say that the pronunciation of *juāllin* is correct according to the Arabic letter. But the Hanafis say that they are correct. It is interesting to note that no one knows the meaning of the word, but they think that if the word is not appropriately pronounced the prayer will not be properly performed.

The next point is about the pronunciation of *āmin*, softly or loudly. The villagers say that the significance behind the loud pronunciation of *āmin* was that, originally men at the back rows of the congregation would go away from the line before they completed their *nāmāj*. In order to prevent this, there was instituted the loud utterance of the word *āmin* so that the *imām* (priest) would know that all the faithful were still there at the end of the *nāmāj*. For this reason, the Mohammadis of Mohānandākhāli maintain the tradition.

Besides these, at the time of *ākāmat* (a part of prayer) the Hanafis raise the hands slightly above the ears and at this time they touch the ear. Then they cross arms over the waist. The Mohammadis raise the hands in the same way but they do not touch ears. They cross arms over the chest. The Mohammadis say that this tradition came about in the early period of Islam when those who had not accepted Islam completely kept their idols under their armpits during the prayer. So they did not cross the hands high on the chest for fear of the idols falling down. They told that the Hanafis are still following that practices.

In relation to *tārābih nāmāj* (prayer is performed at night during the Islamic month of Ramjan) we find discrimination among the Muslims of different mojhab. The people belonging to Mohammadi mojhāb say *tarabih namaj* usually with eight or twelve *rākāts* (step of prayer). On the other hand, the people of Hanafi mojhab perform *tārābih nāmāj* with twenty *rākāts*. The reason is that once the Prophet himself performed *tārābih nāmāj* with eight or twelve *rākāts*, but most of the time he used to perform it with more than twelve.

Hazrat Omar's supported to have told his people to say *tārābih nāmāj* with twenty *rākāts*, and he announced this is the best. From then the people of Hanafi mojhāb observed it regularly and it was supported by the *sāhābis* (religious scholars with Prophet). Later on, it was declared as *sunnat-e-mukāddam* (necessary). The people of Hanafi mojhāb believe that the hadith which is followed by Mohammadis is *jāif* (week). On the other hand, the hādith followed by the Hanafi is *mashur* (strong), because in the *tārābih nāmāj* they have included additional *rākāts*.

We find differentiation among the fore-said mojhābs in relation to their performance of *beh-ter nāmāj* (the prayer is performed at night just after the esā prayer). The Prophet used to perform his *beh-ter nāmāj* two ways: sometimes he was found by the sahabis to perform his *beh-ter* nāmāj with a single *rākāt*, but usually he used to say *beh ter* with three *rākāts*. So the people of Mohammadi mojhab say their *beh-ter nāmāj* with single *rākāt* but followers of Imam Abu Hanifa always perform their *beh-ter* nāmāj with three rākāts.

Another distinction that is found among the Muslims is that when they perform their nāmāj they maintain a link by touching each other with their shoulder that means if they do not maintain such a link then an evil spirit may occupy the space in between them and as a result the prayer will not be acceptable to God. On the other hand, the Hanafis do not maintain this view. At the time of the prayer they simply maintain the straight queue and remain alert so that nobody can interfere between two persons. Besides these the Mohammadis do not maintain *Pir-murid*[2] relationship. They believe that it is not in Islam and if any one believes in this system then he will be *khārij* (out) from Islam. But the Hanafis may if they wish maintain *Pir-murid* relationship. The people of Hanafi Mojhāb in Mohānandākhāli believe that without pir a person may not go to *behesth* (heaven). Because the pir can show his murid how to lead his (murid's) life in a right path, and that will lead him to heaven.

On the day of Id-ul-Āzhā and Id-ul-Fitr the Hanafis pray in the separate *id-gāh* (prayer ground) under the leadership of their respective imāms, and on the day of Id-ul-Āzhā the

Hanafis and Mohammadis sacrifice cows and goats in separate places. The Hanafis observe the Milād-un-Nabi or Milād Sharif as the celebration of the Prophet's birth day, and they also observe *Milāds* on any occasion for thanks giving, the completion of a new house, the opening of new shop or starting a new business, a good harvest, passing school examination or a recovering from an illness (Ellickson ; 1972 : 77). After the milād they distribute sweets among the persons present. On the other hand, the Mohammadis do not observe milād in this village as reported by the informants. They think of it as idolatry, the worship of Mohammad. According to their opinion it is *nā-jāej* (proscribed). They do observe the *Fātehā-doāj-dāhām* death anniversary of the Prophet. The Hanafis occasionally offer *sirni* (offering of God) at the mosque after the jummā nāmāj. The Mohammadis reject this practice.

In Mohānandākhāli usually differentiation can be found among Muslims in relation to *Islamic dalils* (documents) which are observed by all Muslims. The people belonging to Mohammadi mojhab three types of dalils, viz, the Qurān, *hādith* and *ejmā*. On the other hand, the people of Hanafi mojhāb observe four types of dalil—the Qurān, hādith, ejmā and keāsh (idea). The keāsh is determined from the above mentioned three types of dalil and those who made keāsh is generally known as *mujtāhid* (researcher). The reason behind the distinction regarding observation of dalil among the Muslims is that the people of Mohammadi mojhāb observe three types of dalil as the Prophet observed. On the contrary, the people of Hanafi mojhāb observe four types of dalil as Abu Hanifa observed. The people of Mohammadi mojhāb say that at any time keāsh can be made by the religious scholars, but these religious scholars are not sāhābis so keāsh is *nā-jāej*. But the Hanafis say that without keāsh a Muslim cannot lead a proper life according to Islamic custom.

Each sect or sub-sect has its own mollāh who leads prayers and they always try to differentiate between the villagers in terms of their sub-sect affiliation. These leaders often accuse sub-sects other than their own of being un Islamic (Islam. 1974 : 85).

Inter-group Differences in Social Interaction

Though the Hanafi and Mohammadi are endogamous Mojhābs, they freely interdine with each other in their homes. But at social ceremonies such as marriage or funeral feasts they do not inter-dine, and Mohammadis do not accept sirni from Hanafis. The sirni is generally distributed at the end of the jummā-nāmā and at this time many Mohammadi children come to the mosque with the Hanafi children to get it. The Mohammadis do not mind this. According to their opinion sirni is neither hārām (forbidden) nor hālāl (acceptable), it is *makruh* (neutral). Sometimes they do not accept the meat of Id-ul-Azhā from Hanafis or if they accept it for the sake of politeness they later on give it a beggar or poor person. Informally, they participate in each other social and ceremonial feasts if they are on close terms.

Inter-mojhāb marriage is prohibited in Mohānandākhāli, although inter-mojhāb widow remarriage is permissible, as for example, Mr. Fulbash Mandal is a Mohammadi married to a Hanafi widow. She was helpless and the villagers did not dispute the marriage. On the other hand, if a member of Hanafi Mojhab tries to marry into a Mohammadi mojhab, there may be politicking (Islam ; 1974 : 85) between the respective groups against the match. Mr. Yanus, a Mohammadi, faced the same problem after his marriage with a Hanafi girl in Mohānandākhāli. The problem was resolved by holding two religious ceremonies with the mollāhs of their respective sub-sects and the bride became a Mohammadi.

In the area under research I studied a case regarding inter-marriage and inter-dining as follows : one Mr. Zahiruddin belonging to the Hanafi mojhāb arranged the wedding of his daughter with a Mohammadi bride-groom. Normally this type of marriage is very rare indeed in rural areas of Bangladesh. That the Mohammadis are more elevated in rank in comparison with the Hanafis is a settled fact in accordance with the joint acquisence of both group. They believe this in the sense that Mohammadis hail from the direction of Prophet. On the contrary the Hanafis are of origin principally converted from the Hindus and consequently they follow the direction of Abu Hanifa. So, the people of

Mohammadi Mojhāb believe that they are superior to the people of Hanafi mojhāb. But there are some special cases where a Mohammadi groom is wedded to a Hanafi bride. This type of hypogamous marriage is often practiced among the Muslims particularly between the Mohammadi and Hanafi Mojhab. I observed in the following case that the bridegroom came to the bride's father's residence with the *borjātri* (bridesman) including their Mollāh. The ceremony commenced solemnly and the bride was converted into his (groom's) subsect by the Mollāh. Then on the basis of their mutual approbation they were wedded together. Even after the wedding was completed the groom and none of his party man did take any food nor even a glass of customary beverage ; this was the most curious event to be noted. The reason they put forward is that if they do not abide by this practice, the *samaj*[3] of the groom may go against them. Then they returned home, and were cordially welcomed as a couple by the *samāj*. On later occasions when the groom at any time visits the bride's father's residence he usually accompanies his wife. It means that the *samaj* may happen to think that he does not at all take any kind of food cooked by his mother-in-law or any members of the family concerned instead he takes food prepared by his wife. This is practically in the fear that if he does not confirm to this there is the possibility of his being ousted by the *samaj*. But informally he takes food cooked by his mother-in-law or by any family members. But it is interesting to note that during my field work or any time in Mohānandākhāli no marriage occurred with the Hanafi boy and the Mohammadi girl.

In a matter of divorce we observe clear cut distinction between the Mohammadis and Hanafis. It was the custom of Arabia during the time of Prophet Mohammad to divorce a wife off and on without any proper reason. The Arabs thought the women were for pleasure only (Tahabi Sharif; Vol. 2, p. 28). Therefore, to stop such practices the Prophet told his *sāhābis* that if a person divorces his wife uttering *tin-tālāk* (three tālāk) it will be considered as single tālāk. But according to Islamic prohibition if a person uttered three tālāk after three consecutive menstruation periods then the divorce will stand valid. Now if we examine the difference in divorce between the two mojhābs, we come to the conclusion that the talak Mohammadis still observe told by the Prophet to his sahabis to stop frequent divorce among the Arabs. The same is true if also the Islamic prohibition of tin-talak until after three consecutive menstrual periods. In Mohānandākhāli Mohammadis still observe this form.

On the other hand, at the time of Hazrat Omar, the administration became more strict regarding divorce among the Muslims. If a Muslim utters tin-talak in the presence of any witness at a time, the divorce will be confirmed. In Mohānandākhāli the Hanafis observe this rules regarding divorce.

Relations Among the Groups

Each group regards itself higher than the other but they freely cooperate in certain social activities. The usual form of address between the people of two mojhābs is by kinship terms. They sometimes participate in each others funeral processions and *jānājā* (pre-funeral prayers). They invite each other to marriage and initiation ceremonies if they have friendly term and they give customary presents in cash or kind. If they are on friendly terms then they share *hukka* and accept *bidis* from each other. In their daily life they help each other in different ways as neighbours, friends and in fictive kin relations i.e. mutual dyadic relationship can be found between the Hanafis and the Mohammadis. Persons of any mojhāb who face problems of agricultural production or litigation or family trouble consult with influential or wiseman in the village irrespective of mojhabs. An instance, Mr. Karim Mandal, a man of Hanafi mojhāb has knowledge about land holdings of the village and many people of Mohammadi mojhāb come to him when they face problems of this sort. They also hire labour at the time of planting, seeding and harvesting from each other. The people of both mjhab occasionally purchase seasonal crops together and sell them when they can realise a good profit. So, partnership stock business can be found among the Muslims irrespective of mojhāb. Besides these, they share neighbourly relationships and responsibilities. Though they are separate sub-sect, they attend the same school and they belong to the same cooperative society. From the secular point of view the position of an individual in the village *bichār* or *sālish* depends on socio-economic condition irrespective of mojhab. In the village among the Muslims of both mojhabs observe *pardā*. But socio-economic status and *pardā* observance are correlated, because only economically well to do families and those who have social position is comparatively high can afford to keep their wives in *pardā* irrespective of mojhāb. They also believe in the practice of widow re-marriage and also adopt the process to re-accept their divorced wives.

From the religious point of view usually relationship can be seen among the Muslims in relation to belief of the five pillars of Islam irrespective of mojhāb. The people of both the mojhab believe in kālemā, confession of faith that there is no God except Allah and Mohammad the Prophet. Namaj, the prayers of five times daily at the specified times. All the people do not accomplish all five prayers every day, though they know that they should, and they admire the faithful performer of prayers. Rojā, fasts from *sobhi sādiq* (before the dawn) to sunset during the Islamic month of Ramjān. Zākāt, a certain percentage of total wealth, which is taken from the rich and is given to the poor and *hajj*, pilgrimage to Mecca in a specified time. Besides these, the people of both the mojhabs believe in the practice of *tabliga*, an organization of men versed in Islam who see their mission as travelling to the ignorant Muslims to teach them regarding Islamic rules and regulations. They also believe in *jihād*, try heart and soul for extreme sacrifice of life in the defence of faith develop on all Muslims.

Process of Development

Most of over developmental activities are rural or village oriented in building up the required infra-structure. But this developmental programme cannot be treated as an independent question divorced from its social bearings—social mobility, organizational and status system, social disorganization and most importantly social differentiation and the process involved therein. In Mohanandakhali also, a multi-sub-sect village (in the context of Islam) the facts and figures which stems out from the study, I conducted, there reveals the same truth. In my research area, with a deep look through into a Muslim community, I observed some trades of inter sub-sect relations. These sorts of conflict and cohesion are existing among the people of different mojhābs and this should be dealt very consciously because they are thought to have far-reaching significance in the policies relating to rural as well as national development. Motivation to development is found to be distorted by the power structure and the nature of power balance among the people belonging to different mojhābs. Here the Muslim sub-sect differs in the degree of access to economic, social and political power which the range of exploitation and domination of one sub-sect by another.

In Mohanandakhali, the Mohammadis are not only numerically prominent but also politically and economically dominant in comparison to Hanafi. They are the people (Mohammadi) mostly involve with the existing plans and programmes for the rural development in this area. Experts of different fields in connection with development usually take temporary shelter when they come to the village with a view to introduce new programmes, or supervision of the existing programmes. Economic institutions like cooperatives and political institutions like village committees or ward committee are represented mostly by the Mohammadis and thus they have formed a vested interest group in the society. The new technology in the field of agriculture demands timely and regular supply of improved innovation package, the advantage of which is greatlysi phoned off by the dominant group. The prevalence of exploitative production relations such as exist in Mohānandākhāli among the Muslims, in one form or another is working towards a low growth potential and also an inequitable distribution of income. These forces are further re-inforced by the power structure both at the grass-root level and the national level as well as by the kinship and factional grouping dominating this rural society. The distribution of pump sets seem to have followed closely with the local political power and patronage leaning. Given the firm structure in Mohanandakhali efficient utilization of the pumps requires formation of groups by farmers. But these groups are dominated by large Mohammadi farmers and either disproportionately greater use of this faculty is made by them or they manage to extract a high rental from small Hanafi farmers using the pump water. Similar phenomenon is also observed in relation to deep and shallow tubewell. Exploitation of small Hanafi farmers through the operation of the credit market is possible because institutional sources provided to them are very insignificant. The Mohammadi farmers with large land holding have greater access to institutional credit. Thus the tenurial status of the farmer may affect his accessibility to different sources of credit particularly the institutional wants. This is also what enable the money-lender and the like to impose upon week Hanafi borrowers very stringent terms of credit. Apart from shrinkage of supply of institutional credit which drives the small or mini Hanafi farmers to non-traditional sources of credit, it helps creation of inequality of wealth in the study area.

Conclusion

In conclusion it can be mentioned that in Mohanandakhali we find caste like group among the Muslims in relation to endogamy and commensality in between the Hanafis and Mohammadis. Besides these, changes are taking place due to the 'modernization' that is, spread of education, technological innovation, transport and communication. Still inter-mojhab marriage is not normally possible but we observed changing attitude towards inter-mojhab marriage which may occur in future among the people of both mojhābs. Pir-murid relationship is declining gradually among the Hanafis. Inter-group prayer is generally performed when the people of both mojhabs go outside their own village or area. But in the case of litigation or conflict between two mojhābs we observed rigid group differentiation and the simmering conflict surface easily.

In the process of development in a multi-sub-sect Muslim community we find sectional i.e. one sided development, because the dominant group both economically and politically gets the maximum benefit. Consequently in a multi-sub-sect Muslim rural community partial development takes place instead of an overall development.

NOTES

1. Mohanandakhali is a medium sized multi-religion, multi-caste and multi-sub-sect village in Rajshahi district which is situated in the northern part of Bangladesh. It is ten miles north of Rajshahi town—nine miles of metalled motorable road and one mile of *katcha* road. The total population of Mohanandakhali during my field work was about 638. Out of the total population 60 per cent were Muslims and 40 per cent Hindus. Among the Muslims 93 per cent were Mohammadi and the rest of 7 per cent were Hanafis. Agriculture is the main economy of the village.
2. *Pir-Murid* : Pir is a Muslim religious scholar and must have spiritual power. Murid is a person who leads his social and religious life under the guidance of his respective pir.
3. *Samaj* : By samaj is meant a group of people living together generally on the basis of kinship, jati, sect, sub-sect, religion, immigration and territory having a common social identity.

SUGGESTED READINGS

Ali, Azher, "Rural Development in Bangladesh; Bangladesh Academy for Rural Development", Comilla, 1975.

Ansari, Ghaus, "Muslim Caste in Uttar Pradesh, Ethnographic and Folk Culture Society", U.P., Lucknow, 1960.

Dube, S.C., "Indian Village", London, Routledge and Kegan Paul, 1955.

Ellickson, Jean, "A Believer Among Believers : The Religious Beliefs, Practices and Meanings in a Village in Bangladesh." Unpublished Ph. D. thesis. Department of Anthropology; Michigan State University, 1972.

Islam, A.K.M. Aminul, A Bangladesh Village : Conflict and Cohesion. Cambridge, Massachusetts, Schenkman Publishing Company, 1974.

Levy, Reuben, "The Social Structure of Islam," Cambridge University Press, 1969.

Long, Norman, "An Introduction to Sociology of Rural Development", Tavistock Publications, London, 1977.

ELEVEN

Trilochan Das

THE SOCIAL, ANTHROPOLOGICAL, AND POLITICAL PHILOSOPHY OF ACHARYA BRAJENDRANATH SEAL

> Ay, let every man and woman and child, without respect of caste or birth, weakness or strength, hear and learn that behind the strong and the weak, behind the high and the low, behind everyone, there is that Infinite Soul, assuring all the infinite possibility and the infinite capacity to become great and good. Let us proclaim to every soul : Arise, arise, awake! Awake from this hypnotism of weakness. None is really weak; the soul is infinite, omnipotent, and omniscient. Stand up, assert yourself, proclaim the God within you, do not deny Him!
>
> —*Swami Vivekananda*

Dr. Seal's London Address (1911) is an important landmark in the history of human civilisation and thought. Here we are encountered with a scientific evaluation of the inter-racial problems ever made by any thinker on earth. Every word, every expression used by Dr. Seal gives palpable proof of his clear thinking, demonstrating at the same time, in no unmistakable terms, enough evidence of his unbiased, philosophical and scientific mind. . . . Addressing the Universal Races Congress, Brajendranath thus demolished, once for all, all traditional, reactionary, chauvinistic, unfriendly, hatred-promoting, self degrading and cowardice-promoting racialistic theories which harp on the rigidity of race-types and which uphold race supremacy, thereby endangering peace on earth.

—*Trilochan Das*

By his message for racial harmony through the scientific interpretation of race and anthropometrical data, Dr. Seal has enabled mankind, once for all, to face the challenges of racism and racial discrimination as are being upheld by the pseudo-scientific world.

—*Trilochan Das*

> Altogether, according to Seal, from the protoman to the nation-State human personality is the continuous theatre of variabilities, fluencies, mobilities and adaptations. There is no place for rigidity of types in the evolution of human races.
>
> —*Benoy K. Sarkar*

> Nationalism is only a halting stage, in the onward march of humanity. Nationalism, imperialism, federationism are world-building forces working often unconsciously and in apparent strife towards the one far-off divine event.
>
> —*B.N. Seal*

> Seal does not appear to be a purely speculative theoretician. He has a practical aim, namely, that of guiding and controlling the future evolution of humanity by conscious selection and intelligent adaptation to the system and procedure of Nature.
>
> —*Benoy K. Sarkar*

> No view of civilization is sound or adequate which considers race and racial types statically and not dynamically as growing, developing, or progressive entities.
>
> —*B.N. Seal*

IT IS NOT known to many that as in many other fields, Acharya Brajendranath Seal (1864-1938) made a distinct contribution to the social, anthropological, and political philosophy. His social, anthropological, and political ideas can be traced back to many of his fragmentary writings, and addresses including some of his letters to Rabindranath Tagore.

Acharya Brajendranath Seal's inaugural address, "the Meaning of Race, Tribe, and Nation", as the opener of the Universal Races Congress, London, 1911;[1] his presidential address at the opening of Rabindranath Tagore's Visva-Bharati, Shantiniketan (1921); his *Reports* as chairman of the Mysore Constitutional Reforms Committee (1922-23), and as chairman of Mysore Committee on State Aid to Industries (1924); his *Advent of Youth* (1924); his presidential address at the Mythic Society (1924); his address on Sri Ramakrishna as the general president of the World Congress of Religions (1936), his *Rammohan—The Universal Man*, his *Quest Eternal* (1936); his Autobiography (Ms.); and last but not the least his *Positive Sciences of the Ancient Hindus* (1915) are invaluable documents where we can discover Brajendranath as a positive and dynamic social, anthropological, and political thinker.

Be it noted at the very outset that Brajendranath's *Reports* as Chairman of the Mysore Constitutional Reforms Committee (1922-23) as well as the Mysore Committee on State Aid to Industries (1924) are valuable documents reflecting his depth of knowledge as a political thinker.

Referring to Brajendranath's *Report* on Mysore Constitutional Reforms, Dr. S. Radhakrishnan, the former President of India, stated that Dr. Seal prepared a very important document on the administrative reforms of the Mysore government. He made some original suggestions regarding the constitutional reforms in our country. In fact, the Mysore Constitutional Reforms suggested by Dr. Seal gave complete satisfaction to one and all. Here, one is struck wonder by being encountered with Dr. Seal's depth of knowledge of political science, including constitutional law, and his wonderful ability and experience in administration as well.

Indeed, the Maharaja of Mysore was so much impressed by Brajendranath's knowledge on political affairs, and his distinct contribution as a political thinker as well, that the Maharaja appointed Brajendranath as an Additional Member of the Mysore State Government and had no peace of mind until his Government could confer on Brajendranath the highly coveted and unique title of *Rajtantrapravin*, i.e., an adept in state-craft or state-polity. Brajendranath, on his part, rose equally to the occasion by proving himself to be not only a giant political thinker, but a great statesman and an able administrator as well.

It is interesting to note in this connection that the Universal Races Congress was held in 1911 at London.

The Congress sought to "discuss in the light of science and the modern conscience the general relations subsisting between the peoples of the West and those of the East, between so-called white and so-called coloured peoples, with a view to encouraging between them a fuller understanding, the most friendly feeling, and heartier cooperation".

In the true spirit of the aims and objectives set forth by the organisers of the London Congress, Brajendranath, as the opener of the Universal Races Congress, made a distinct contribution to world thought by presenting his paper, "The Meaning of Race, Tribe and Nation".

At the very outset, let us stress the fact that Brajendranath's London address is of great significance; in fact, it is an important landmark in the history of human civilization and thought. Here we encounter with one of the best scientific evaluations of inter-racial problems ever made by any thinker. Every word and every expression used gives palpable proof of his clear thinking, demonstrating at the same time, in no unmistakable terms, enough evidence of his unbiased, philosophical, and scientific mind.

As a matter of fact, in the context of present-day controversy regarding the advocacy of the genetic theory supporting the inequality of races, Dr. Seal's address has acquired new dimensions. As Prof. Sisir Kumar Ghose of the Visva Bharati University has aptly put it, Brajendranath's address was indeed "a confession of faith in racial harmony and intellectual fellowship, an idea which he would repeat later in his inaugural address before Tagore's educational centre, Visva Bharati".

The controversy which is deeply influencing racial policies has been recently revived in Britain, thus creating an embarrassing situation and involving an eminent Nobel Laureate. The controversy arose from the theory propounded by Dr. Arthur Jensen of California University who, in his report published in the *Harvard Educational Review* in 1969, produced statistics to show that American Negroes have an average 15 per cent. lower I.Q. than American Whites, and then said this proved the argument that intelligence was influenced more by inheritance than by environmental factors.[2]

Prof. Jensen's argument was supported by Prof. H.J. Eysenck of London University, who advanced the argument by his analysis of Irish, Jewish, and English I.Q.s. The controversy is still rocking the academic circles in the West, and has been used by some politicians and educationists to justify their racial views or for advocating segregation in educational institutions.

It is against this context that the Conservative Liberal, Lord Boyle, Vice-Chancellor of the Leeds University, has been involved. The fact is that the Leeds University recently offered an Honorary Doctorate to Prof. William Shockley, Head of the Engineering Science Department of Stanford University in California and Nobel Laureate for the invention of the transistor 25 years ago, but has now discovered that Prof. Shockley is an ardent advocate of the genetic theory of the inequality of races. Further, Prof. Shockley has advocated the sterilization of people with low I.Q., which has also racial implications.

Leeds University asked Prof. Shockley that, in order to avoid further controversy, he should decline the Doctorate and relieve Leeds University of implicitly approving of the genetic theory. When Prof. Shockley refused to do so, Leeds University withdrew the offer :

> Prof. Shockley has said he would exploit the Leeds episode to stress that it was frightened of research which is all that he says he wants on the factors that make up intelligence in human beings.[3]

Toeing the arguments of Dr. Jensen, Prof. Eysenck, and Prof. Shockley, Prof. John R. Baker has, in his publication, *Race*, held that "Parents of very low cognitive ability would be likely not only to provide poorer home environments than others, but also to transmit their low cognitive ability to their offspring".[4] Thus, to believe Prof. Baker, a fool's son must be a fool ! According to him, "transmission of cognitive ability" is genetic. But this is absolutely wrong; apart from hereditary influences, cognitive ability is acquired in particular social, cultural, and environmental settings. Nutrition also has no mean role to play in this respect. Baker's thesis has done a great disservice to great humanistic ideals, bringing joy to the racists in South Africa, the United States, and elsewhere.

In his "Lettre ouverte aux parents des petits écoliers"[5] ("Open Letter to the Parents of School Children"), Prof. Debray-Ritzen has pinned his faith in tests, measurements, statistics, intellect, biology, etc. To him, therein lies the absolute guarantee for truth. The inequality of intelligence, of "genetic" origin, can be "scientifically", measured by the I.Q. This is confirmed at the school and by social success. Prof. Debray-Ritzen has therefore asserted that the egalitarian myth is criminal.

Presenting a rigorous and bold analysis of the problem, Theodosius Dobzhansky has maintained, "We may think that the best way of discrediting the idea of equality is to prove that men are genetically—and hence irremediably—different. Therefore human equality depends on the rights and sacred character of every human being and not on his physical or mental characteristics".[6] There are differences amongst individuals even at the time of birth. Statistics tend to prove that members of unfavoured social groups (e.g., the poor and the Blacks of the U.S.A.) have, on an average, much lower I.Q. than the Whites and the rich.

Even while accepting the validity of these postulates, Dobzhansky has recalled the fact that Scarr-Salapatec proved in 1971, by studying several groups of black and white twins, that heredity is not a factor independent of environment. These two factors act and react on each other, are inter-dependent, and change reciprocally. The genetic conditioning of intelligence itself varies, depending on the *milieu*. These are not only the social effects of the hereditary characteristics which are transformed by environment, but the possibility also for those genetic data to be manifested.[7]

Such views are a "breach of U.N. and Commonwealth declarations which denounce racial discrimination of any kind". These educationists have rightly been accused of having done both science and society a disservice by upholding such notions and encouraging a positive threat to world peace.

The *National Herald*, in an editorial article, rightly observed, "Apartheid is a crime against humanity and it should stir the conscience of mankind"; and world opinion has been called upon to go on "registering its protest till the last vestige of racial discrimination is eradicated".[8] Referring to the fact that at the close of its Twentieth Session, in December, 1965, the International Convention on the Elimination of All Forms of Racial Discrimination was adopted by the U.N. General Assembly, the *National Herald* editorial article has boldly put forward the following proposition:

> Racism involves the assertion that inequality is absolute and unconditional, which means that a race is inherently and by its very nature superior or inferior to others, quite independently of the physical conditions of the habitat and social factors. But this is an erroneous and unjust approach. The contention that a white man is superior to a black man is as absurd as the contention that a white horse will be faster than a black one.

Addressing the Universal Races Congress, Brajendranath demolished all traditional, reactionary, chauvinistic, unfriendly, hatred-promoting, self-degrading, and cowardice-promoting racialistic theories which harp on the rigidity of race-types and which uphold race supremacy, thereby endangering peace on earth.

In his scientific analysis of *Race, Tribe, and Nation*, there is no room for racial discrimination, and hence apartheid has been disapproved, repudiated, and virtually condemned. This is rather a clarion call for condemning and banning all such inhuman discriminatory practices.

Asserting that there was no place for rigidity of types in the evolution of human races, Brajendranath observed that from the proto-man to the nation-state human personality was a continuous theatre of variabilities, fluencies, mobilities, and adaptations. Race and race-types are also dynamically growing, developing, and progressive entities. Thus the proto-man "possessed a phylogenetic variability" ; he was a "plastic and progressive being, not arrested and not decadent, as savages in many cases have come to be in their isolated and inhospitable habitats".

According to Dr. Seal, "In the tribal organization also, described as 'ethnic civilization' or cultural races by Ratzel, the human capacities are 'like all other bio-sociological characters, plastic, fluent, and developable under suitable conditions and stimuli' ".

Discussing the sociological interpretation of anthropometrical data presented by Brajendranath, Dr. Benoy Sarkar has stated :

> According to Seal the flexibility, plasticity, and developability of the human capacities are continued through the

> subsequent stages of social evolution, for instance, in the "national race" stage. In this stage the elements of the previous ethnic or tribal stage are but redistributed. The "increasing variability of response in the individual" is described as the cause and concomitant of individual emancipation from the family and clan. Along with this is likewise developed "the increasing variability of the social mind and the phenomenon of social choice".[9]

Maintaining that the fallacy of other racialism lies in the conception of the rigidity or permanence of race-types or culture-types, Brajendranath has observed :

> Most of the morphological distinctions (head and nose forms, etc.) do not connote vitality or a high or low place in the normal scale of development. The head and the foot do not vary among races according to their order of superiority. Then Dr. Seal has clearly asserted, "A long head (a so-called simian character) or a long foot is not a characteristic of inferiority." He has further observed that "both morphological and physiological characters change with change of environment".

According to Brajendranath morphological characters, e.g., the structure of the hair, the face, the orbits, the nose, the cranium, and the pelvis are not so stable as some physical anthropologists would fain believe. Again, "The cephalic index in man, even if it were not otherwise open to dispute as confounding real distinctions of shape, seems to be unstable under special conditions".

Arguing that the psycho-social character (and therefore the racial types of man) are marked by that greater range, variability and plasticity of response (i.e., of the internal factor in organic evolution) which is the concomitant of all higher and more complex organization, Brajendranath observed :

> No view of civilization is sound or adequate which considers race and racial types statically and not dynamically as growing, developing of progressive entities.

Be it stressed once more that Brajendranath's remark "both morphological and physiological characters change with change of evironment," is highly significant. Not only that there is no place for rigidity of types in the evolution of human races, which are dynamically flexible, plastic, variable, and developing ; the human personality is also the continuous theatre of variabilities, fluencies, mobilities, and adaptations. Dr. Benoy K. Sarkar has thus rightly observed :

> Seal's observations that "both morphological and physiological characters change with change of environment is well calculated to take the edge of all racialistic theories which harp on the rigidity of race-types".

We are confronted here with Brajendranath's genetic view of race, viz., genetic anthropology. He has tried to harmonize the conflicting claims of (1) physical anthropology, with its permanent anatomical types, (2) cultural ethnology, with its geographical zones of ethnic culture, and (3) the philosophy of history with its law of three or more stages. As Dr. Sarkar has said, "A synthetic view of race is possible, according to him, when we consider it not as a statistical but as a dynamical entity, plastic, fluent, growing, with energies not exhausted. This is what he calls genetic anthropology. It studies races and racial types as radicals, their growth and transmutation into ethnic cultural units (classes, tribes, peoples), and finally the course of their evolution into historic nationalities".

Dr. Seal's above analysis in the light of science and modern conscience has not only demolished the age-old, traditional, conception of race supremacy ; it is at the same time calculated to combat colour prejudice, the forcible shutting of the door in the West against the East, the forcible breaking open of the East in favour of the West, national chauvinism, mutual aggressiveness, and war.

Brajendranath thus largely fulfilled the aims and objectives put forward by the London Congress. Indeed Dr. Seal's statement that "both morphological and physiological characters change with change of environment" deserves to be closely studied. We are reminded, in this connection, of Brajendranath's observations on heredity and sex as discussed in Chapter VI of his *Positive Sciences of the Ancient Hindus.*[10]

Discussing the traditional conception that specific parental characters are transmitted to the offspring, Brajendranath took note of the fact that "Charaka assumes that the sperm-cell of the male parents contains minute elements derived from each of its organs or tissues". He also noted that Sankara similarly stated that the sperm-cell represented "in miniature every organ of the parent organism, and contains in potential the whole organism that is developed out of it". Questioning the above views, Brajendranath observed that if the above views are true, then "Why are not congenital deformities of the parent, or constitutional diseases contained in later life, invariably inherited?" He further observed, "Congenital blindness, deafness, dumbness, stammering, lameness, or deformity of the spinal column or of the bony framework, dwarfish stature, or constitutional diseases like madness, leprosy, or skin diseases in the parent, do not necessarily produce corresponding deformities or infirmities in the offspring".

Dr. Seal has further noted that the fertilised ovum is composed of elements which arise from the whole parental organism, but it is not the developed organs of the parents, with their idiosyncracies or acquired characters that determine or contribute the elements of the sperm-cell. The parental germ-plasm contains the whole parental organism in miniature no doubt, but it is independent of the parents' developed organs, and it is not necessarily affected by their idiosyncracies or deformities. In fact, the parental germ-plasm is an organic whole independent of the developed parental body and its organs.

Atreya and Charaka have also emphasised, "the influence of abundant or defective nutrition, and of the constituents of the food, etc., on the characters of the Vija in the reproductive tissue, specially as regards sexual characters, the stature, and the colour-pigment" of the offspring. Thus nutrition has a great role to play not only in determining the stature and the colour pigment; nutrition also determines the sex. Thus, ghee and milk for the male, and oil and beans for the female parent, are favourable to the "seed". As such the role of heredity becomes limited, enabling the environment to play its own dominant role in the process of the evolution and development of the human, racial, or even individual characteristics.

The reason why Brajendranath emphasized that "both morphological and physiological characters change with change of environment" now becomes abundantly clear.

Be it noted in this connection that in Dr. Seal's scientific analysis of race and culture, the dynamic process of the individual man and society has a distinct role to play. In his analysis, the hereditary or stable characters are subjected to the intelligent adaptation of the environment, and finally the conscious social selection acts upon them. Thus Dr. Seal has considered the race and racial types not statically but dynamically, as growing, developing, progressive entities—plastic, fluent, growing, with energies not exhausted—the human personality being the continuous theatre of variabilities, fluencies, mobilities, mutabilities, flexibilities, adaptations, etc.

Endorsing Dr. Seal's sociological interpretation of anthropometrical data, Dr. Benoy K. Sarkar, himself a noted anthropologist and sociologist, has pointed out :

> The fallacy of Nordicism as of other racialism lies in the conception of the rigidity or permanence of race-types or culture-types. But the evidences of physical as well as cultural anthropology point to racial as well as cultural mutabilities or flexibilities.

Indeed, it is heartening to note that following the footsteps of Sir Brajendranath Seal, the United Nations has been continuing in its most persistent efforts against racism, racial discrimination, and racial persecution, which goes back to 1946. The International Convention on the Elimination of All Forms of Racial Discrimination was adopted by the General Assembly in 1964. The General Assembly proclaimed in November, 1973, a Decade for Action "to promote human rights and fundamental freedoms for all, without distinction of any kind on grounds of race, colour, descent, or national or ethnic origin, specially by eradicating racial prejudice, racism and racial prejudice, racism and racial discrimination". The U.N. Convention on the Suppression and Punishment of the Crime of Apartheid, which declared apartheid a crime against humanity, came into force in 1976. It is also interesting to note that the World Conference to Combat Racism and Racial Discrimination, held in August, 1978, at Geneva, was mainly concerned with reviewing the progress of the U.N. campaign against racism, racial discrimination, and apartheid.

In this context, it would not be totally out of place to take note of Dr. Seal's observations on the state of anthropological studies in India about 1910. Referring to the state of anthropological measurements in India, Dr. Seal stated :

> Unfortunately, the anthropological measurements in India, on the physical side, are vitiated by the double error : the measurements are certainly desultory and haphazard, and the statistical method is of the crudest arithmetical kind, absolutely unsuited to mixed stocks giving rise to complex and variable curves. The result has been that in place of the old Puranic accounts of 36 castes or 108 or more sub-castes evolving by permutation and combination of an original four, we have the new Purana of the Blue books on Indian Castes and Tribes, of which Sir Herbert Risley was the prolific *Vyasa.*

Presenting a scientific analysis of race origins in the Indian Peninsula, Dr. Seal's analytical study deserves to be quoted as follows :

> We must study the question of race origins in the Peninsula. The old haphazard comparison and the old anthropometry without scientific or statistical technique, have left us in a quandary. We do not know how many distinct races, pure or mixed, there are in the Peninsula, we do not know the blends or compositions in the mixed varieties, and we wander from the Australian Bushes to the Ugrian Steppes, in search of our fatherland, like Japhet in search of a father. Now it is within the bounds of our existing scientific technique to answer the first two questions, which are the most fundamental ones. And when the distinct South Indian types have been fixed, the affinity of any of these types with Papuan or Australian, with the Sakai or the Semang, can also be proved or disproved by the same technique. To take a significant case, much is made of Schmidt and Pater's brilliant hypothesis of the Mon Khmer

races, and of their Austral and other divisions, for whom congeners have been claimed among some South Indian as well as Assamese tribes. I have applied statistical methods to this widely accepted conclusion, and found the anthropological evidence distinctly against this bold and sweeping hypothesis. As for our Akkadian and Sumerian affinities, physical, linguistic and cultural, they cannot be put to any anthropometric tests, *pace* painted head forms, but in any case, Mesopotamia will ever remain a comfortable word. Then there are certain facts which have been brought out by the anthropometrical surveys as regards two broad divisions, the first comprising the Tulus, Canarese and Telegus, and the second the Tamil and the Malayalam classes, of which the former, under supposed Scythian influences from the north, are sub-brachycephalic or mesaticephalic, and the latter, supposed to be Dravidian man, are dolichocephalic or sub-dolichocephalic. Similarly, the nasal index shows a certain gradation from the long and narrow to the short and broad type, as we proceed from the Brahman through the Tamil Paraiyan to the Paniyan. The pigment of the skin and the orbital index also show a similar gradation. Of course, figures always admit of serial arrangement of gradation, but the remarkable thing is that in a broad way, the more marked census divisions tend to differ from one another, not by a single index, but by an ensemble of indices, cephalic, nasal, orbital and dermal. Several lines of investigation by the new methods are therefore suggested. After taking correct measurements, it has to be seen how far the marks are stable, whether the separate indices are highly correlated, and whether the intervals separating the groups constitute statistically significant differences, which is the crux of the matter. Next comes a still more difficult inquiry : whether for each of the divisions, the curve of indices for any single character can be broken up into two curves, one of convergent evolution under the influence of a common environment and the needs of a common adaptation, and the other a curve showing either a pure type or a mixed type due to racial fusion and inter-mixture. It may be noted that in Northern India we can trace the same grada-

> tion, though not one so sure or so uninterrupted, nor, to the same extent, in ensembles of characters, as we proceed from Cashmere and the Punjab to Northern and Eastern Bengal : the direction, both in the Continent and the Peninsula, is from the North-West to the South-East. The facts seem to point both to convergence and to fusion, but only the new biometric methods are of any avail in such investigations.[11]

Pointing out that "India offers the grandest example of ethnic and cultural fusion", Dr. Seal then observed ;

> The Indian peoples, cultures, and cults offer us examples partly of stratification, partly of mosaic cementing, and partly of blend and fusion. The evolution of a composite man and a composite civilization is the central and abiding fact of Indian history. In physical or cultural types, in folk instincts and social postulates, in styles or conventions of art, in myth, tradition and dogma, even in the very language that is the vehicle of thought, and in the structural form of that thinking itself, India offers the grandest example of ethnic and cultural fusion, though the experiment has not always been successful; witness the physical segregation or isolation of certain primitive stocks, and cultures that have not yet successfully assimilated. To the man of science, India offers transitions of cultures and presents the strata with sufficient distinctions to study the dynamic process of man and his culture in the making.

The concluding remarks of Dr. Seal are worth recording here :

> To the historian, this supreme fact of a composite culture lays down the ground-plan, the pattern, of Indian history. A mere side-view of that history, Brahmanical, Buddhist or Jaina—Aryan, Dravidian or Kolarian—Rajput, Moghul or Occidental, is no history at all. The epic of Indian history must, like the Ramayana, tell the story of a great cooperation between North and South, between East and West, between Aryan and Dravidian, between civilized and jungle man, for a great consummation, and this story will point the way to the greater epic of humanity.

As a Political and Social Thinker

In his same paper on "The Meaning of Race, Tribe, and Nation" presented to the London Congress, Brajendranath defined the nation as follows :

> A nation is a conscious social personality exercising rational choice as determined by a scheme of ideal ends or values, and having an organ, the State, for announcing and executing its will.

According to Brajendranath all members of a truly national state are integral members of this composite personality. But they are not all merged in the national State. The individual units are themselves persons and therefore determining. As Dr. Benoy Sarkar observed :

> An important point in Seal's position is indicated below. The State furnishes a common bondship of a new denomination. All the bonds of common descent or kinship, common religion, common social customs, common personal law, consumer cultural state, even a common language, are rendered superfluous and indeed replaced by the new bond created or implied by the State. As a corollary, Seal may be taken to admit the existence of diverse races, cultures etc. in a national state.

Another significant aspect in Brajendranath's political ideology deserves to be specially noted. In his ideology, the existence of theocratic codes, servile classes, ethnic disabilities, privileged orders, and co-ordinated jurisdictions (ecclesiastical, feudal, or municipal) retard the free and normal development of a "national race," the nation or national personality. Hence in his conception, all these "ethnic survivals disappeared in adult nationality". As Dr. Sarkar states :

> Law is described as nothing but the standing will of the national personality. In the regime of the national going as contrasted with that of the ethnic the old and customary law receives its sanction explicitly or implicitly from the will. According to Seal the nation is the higher, i.e., the

> developed stage in an evolution from the protoman upwards. The tribe represents an intermediate station or stations in this upward march of the human group.

In Dr. Seal's conception, the societal evolution does not, however, stop at the national personality. Dr. Seal has gone one step further. Thus, "Nationalism is only a halting stage in the onward march of humanity. Nationalism, imperialism, federationism are world-building forces working often unconsciously and in apparent strife towards the one far-off divine event".[12]

The goal of the entire evolution is a "realised universal humanity with an organic and organised construction".

> Seal's ideology makes of him a Kin of the pre-1914 internationalists of Eur-America.
>
> —*Benoy Sarkar*

Speaking in 1938 at the Bangiya Samaj Vijnan Parishat (Bengali Institute of Sociology), Calcutta, on Dr. Seal's Political Ideas, Prof. Benoy Sarkar rightly observed :

> Seal does not appear to be a purely speculative theoretician. He has a practical aim, namely, that of guiding and controlling the future evolution of humanity by conscious selection and intelligent adaptation to the system and procedure of Nature. To this applied philosophy of politics he comes by the historical study of race-developments, the genetic method.... [He] would like to see the establishment of a world's Humanity League in order to promote mutual understanding amongst members of different races, peoples, and nationalities. The propaganda comprises the endowment of professorships in the universities of East and West. He is interested likewise in the devising of measures calculated to combat colour prejudice, the forcible shutting of the door in the West against the East, the forcible breaking it open in the East in favour of the West, national chauvinism, mutual aggressiveness, and war.

Making further a critical appraisal of Brajendranath's

political ideas, Prof. Benoy Sarkar made the following observations :

> Seal's analysis of the nation or national personality, meritorious as it is on several grounds noted above, appears to be defective, however, in several particulars. First, it takes the entire post-tribal stage of evolution as one uniform process. The history of all the historical states since the earliest times becomes virtually one homogeneous stage. In the second place, Seal's presentation of the national personality and the national will fails to bring out the anti-thesis between people and people on political grounds. The situations created by the government of one people by another people are not explained by him. The analysis cannot throw any light on the nationality movement, the growth of nationalism, etc. in modern times from Washington, Herder, Fichte, Mazzini, and Renan to Aurobindo, Masaryk, and Hitler. The problems envisaged by Seal are consequently less comprehensive and realistic than those of Hobhouse (*Social Evolution and Political Theory*, 1911). And of course they are entirely different from those in the present author's *Science of History* (London, 1912), and the *Politics of Boundaries*, Vol. I (1926), in which the nations or nation-states of history are examined in their inter-statal relations without reference to their racial or tribal origins.[13]

Be that as it may, in his attempt to evaluate Brajendranath strictly as a political scientist, Dr. Benoy Sarkar has chiefly limited his discussion on the political ideas of Brajendranath to his London Address (1911). As such, in his discussion, Dr. Benoy Sarkar has ignored Brajendranath's many other fragmentary writings, including his hitherto unpublished autobiography and some of his other writings, wherefrom we can trace some of the significant social and political ideas of Brajendranath, his role as a prophet of World Peace and his plea for universal cosmic humanism.

The First World War (1914-1918) shook the world and the destructions that took place, bringing untold miseries to thousands and thousands of individual men, women, and their families, deeply moved Sir Brajendranath Seal. Brajendranath was then thoroughly seized with the problems of maintaining peace on earth. He could justly realise that peace was essentially needed for the problem-ridden and thickly-crowded individualistic life of Europe, since all the social problems accumulated in the war-torn and highly sophisticated western hemisphere. There is no wonder therefore that Brajendranath was mainly concerned with the problems of peace on earth. When invited by Rabindranath Tagore to preside over the foundation ceremony of the Visva Bharati, Shantiniketan, in 1921, he stressed again and again the need for world peace and disarmament. Acharya Brajendranath said :

> There is need for a religious movement of new humanism for simultaneous universal disarmament of all nations.[14]

Seized as Brajendranath was with the problem of International peace, he advocated, "International peace can only be ensured if there be fellowship of one man with the other". He was firmly convinced that political efforts alone were not sufficient for fostering peace on earth.

Dr. Seal further pointed out, "Individual salvation alone will not do in the modern times. There is no salvation, unless there is salvation for one and all". He reminded us that "There is always a vast idea of freedom in Hinduism—that wonderful speciality of Hindu have a greater responsibility to offer that ideal to the Universe".

Dr. Seal also referred to the fact that "India always stood for non-violence, fraternity, and peace". He added :

> India has sought that peace with the idea of discovering the universal outlook in every individual and to feel the unity of the Brahman in the same. He further realized that by establishing "universalism, we shall know ourselves and shall give our message to the world.

In fact, Brajendranath was one in thought with Rabindranath, and both of them thought that India should become the meeting point of the East and the West.

Referring to the East-West collaboration, Brajendranath stated, "As we have to accept the centralization and organization of the State from Europe, so we have also to give the group principle to Europe".

Brajendranath further maintained that there was a greater unity of human race even in this diversity. While dealing with the question of political evolution, Dr. Seal pointed out, "Economics with statistics must furnish the basic ideas on which our political life has to be built".

Dr. Seal continued, "But the economic life is not everything. Equality and equity are the fundamental concepts which must be the ultimate ruling ideas, and what must be aimed at is that each individual must count for one, and nobody for less than one or more than one. On this basis must be reared all political life of which the ruling idea is cooperation, though non-violent non-cooperation may be resorted to temporarily as a corrective, but never as an ultimate end".

In no unmistakable terms, Dr. Seal stressed the ultimate fundamental and inalienable right of the individual. Dr. Seal thus reminded us :

> But all this is subject to the recognition of every individual's ultimate, fundamental and inalienable right, that of civil liberty, which may be summed up under the five ultimate principles—freedom of movement, freedom of speech, freedom of association, freedom of press, and the freedom of preaching (or prophesying).

In his last message to the people in April, 1938, Dr. Seal referred to the fact that "In India, it is not merely the individual and the State that are the ruling factors ; the community or social group has an independent life and value which sometimes overrides the requirements and ideals of the individual and the State".

Dr. Seal's clarion call to Indians, irrespective of caste, creed or provincial affiliations, to forget their petty differences and to devote their energy to evolving one common nationality—the Indian nationality—is worth recalling. Indeed, long before India's independence, long before the Indian leaders started thinking of evolving a secular state, Acharya Brajendranath Seal pleaded for the emergence of a common Indian nationality. In replying to the Jayanti felicitations in December 1935, Dr. Seal gave his message as follows.

> My last days are embittered by one thought: the wranglings of those who as the children of India should be bound by ties of brotherhood and friendship. Remember that Hindu or Moslem, Christian or Sikh, you can fulfil the best in your religion by a spirit of give and take, by giving out of your abundance and taking in a spirit of sincere amity and goodwill. *All that is merely sectarian and communal must yield to the spirit of a common nationality, and nationality itself must be fulfilled in one common brotherhood of man in Universal Humanity.*

Visualizing India's supreme role as a propounder of a new gospel of freedom in a strife-torn modern civilised world, Acharya Brajendranath Seal made the correct appraisal when he reminded us, "A world gone mad and clanking the chains in hymns of hate, looks and looks not in vain, to the East, nay to India, for a new gospel of freedom, a gospel of the peace of the spirit, in the oneness of the Brahman".

Incidentally, Dr. Seal's presidential address to the Mythic Society in Bangalore, 1924, is a masterpiece which showed the savant as a master-interpreter of India's cultural forces that were at work. Dr. Seal gave abundant evidence how his mind was engaged in acting as a cementing force between the North and the South—between Dravidian culture and Aryan culture. He pleaded for "a great cooperation between North and South, between East and West, between Aryan and Dravidian, between civilized and jungle man, for a great consummation, and this story will point the way to the greater epic of humanity".

We could have entered into further discussion in details of the social, anthropological, and political ideas of Brajendranath, had we been able to have at least a glimpse of Dr. Seal's Autobiography. Unfortunately, his Autobiography is practically inaccessible, being still in manuscript form ; but an examination of the contents enables us to establish the fact that Brajendranath was not only seized with the social problems in India and strongly pleaded for social reforms ; he was equally concerned with the future political and constitutional set-up in India. He also discussed patriarchal and matriarchal forms of society. Brajendranath even gave his thought to the Jewish problem ; he equally entered into discussion on Islamic religious scripture since the seventh century and the contributions of the Muslims.

Again, the ideals of the East and the West did not escape his attention. War was viewed as some sort of a disease. Also, topics like New Ways of Resistance, Evolution *v*. Revolution, History of Human Evolution, Humanity, etc. all made their own, irresistible appeal to Brajendranath, who could become a man with encyclopaedic knowledge because of his all-embracing interests. Be it noted also that Brajendranath was equally distressed by social calamities and social injustices. He prophesied that the social and political life of India in the twenty-first century would be influenced by the backward classes and the scheduled castes. He wanted the caste, class, creed, and race distinctions, as well as the distinctions between the rich and the poor, to be abolished. In fact, he was full of sympathy for the down-trodden millions.

In Dr. Seal's social philosophy, youth occupy an enviable position. Suffice it to say that Brajendranath had firm faith in the potentialities of youth "working to construct the world afresh from the mass of ruined debris". He thus paid glowing tributes to the youth who also were capable of self-immolating service with a smiling countenance and were "the inheritor(s) of a transcendental sphere".[15]

A titan of titans, Brajendranath further dreamt "beautiful dreams of renovated man". He had an optimistic message for the individual man and woman whom he would like to be free from the bonds of Law and Nature, emerging as the devotees of Truth and Freedom. In his *Quest Eternal*, Dr. Seal chanted "the law of man's deliverance", and sang the song of "the just man militant. . . . A new Prometheus, Universal man".[16]

Incidentally, let us not lose sight of the fact that Brajendranath had full sympathy with the patriotic aspirations of young Bengal and was, in fact, one of the leading guiding angels of the glorious Bengali revolution of 1905. He was also a great votary of world peace and a prophet of cosmic humanism as well.

Brief Biographical Note

Sir Brajendranath Seal the great savant-philosopher was born in Calcutta on 4 December, 1938, and as a child showed signs of being a prodigy. It is known that even as a student he gave initiation to Swami Vivekananda in philosophic studies.

After a brilliant academic career he taught at various colleges in Bengal and elsewhere before being appointed as Vice-Chancellor of Mysore University.

Dr. Seal shot to world fame by delivering the Inaugural Address at the International Congress of Orientalists held at Rome in 1899, where he presented as many as four papers marked for their originality and distinct scholarship.

It's encyclopaedic mind and catholic outlook enabled him to contribute to varied fields of study. The versatility of his genius invoked these comments from Carveth Reed himself: "... the deep unfathomable learning of this Bengali Savant and his encyclopaedic knowledge have struck me with wonder". Perhaps one might end this note with Seal's own words which well express his life's credo :

I would rather burn than renegade turn,
The right to Peace and Hope thus earn,
And Truth and Freedom miss

NOTES

1. B.N. Seal, "Meaning of Race, Tribe and Nation," in *Inter-Racial Problems*, edited by G. Spiller, London, 1911.
2. Arthur Jensen, in *Harvard Educational Review*, 1969.
3. V.R. Bhatt, *Hindusthan Times* (18 Feb. 1973).
4. John R. Baker, *Race*, Oxford University Press, London, 1974.
5. Pierre Debray-Ritzen, "Lettre ouverte aux parents des petits écoliers" Albin Michel.
6. Theodosius Dobzhansky, *Le Droit a l'Intelligence: Génétique et Egalité*, (Editions Complexe, Bruxelles).

7. Norbert Bensaid, "L'écrémeur de tetes", *Le Nouvel Observateur*, No. 731, (Nov. 13-19, 1978), pp. 59-60.
8. *National Herald* (29 Aug. 1968).
9. Benoy, K. Sarkar, *The Political Philosophies Since 1905*, Vol. II, Part III, (1942), p. 80.
10. B.N. Seal, *Positive Sciences of the Ancient Hindus*, Longmans, Green & Co., London, 1915.
11. *Quarterly Journal of the Mythic Society*, (October, 1924) pp. 11-12.
12. *In Inter-Racial Problems*, (ed.) by G. Spiller, London, 1911, pp. 10-13.
13. Benoy Kumar Sarkar, *The Political Philosophies Since 1905*, Vol. II, Part I, 1942, pp. 250-254.
14. B.N. Seal, Presidential Address, Shantiniketan, 1921.
15. B.N. Seal, *Advent of Youth*, 1924.
16. B.N. Seal, *Quest Eternal*, 1936.

SUGGESTED READINGS

Bhatt, V.R., *Hindusthan Times*, Feb. 18, 1973.

Baker, John R., *Race*. Oxford University Press, London, 1974.

Bensaid, Norbert. "L'écrémeur de têtes". *Le Nouvel Observateur*, no. 731, Nov. 13-19, 1978, pp. 54-60.

Das Gupta Punya Priya, World Conference against Racism. *Indian Express*, August 21, 1978.

Debray-Ritzen, Pierrè, "Lettre ouverte aux parents des petits écoliers", Albin Michel

Dobzhansky, Theodosius, *Le Droit a l'Intelligence* : *Génétique et Egalité*, Editions Complexe, Bruxelles.

Jensen, Arthur, *Harvard Educational Review*, 1969.

National Herald, Editorial, August 29, 1968.

Sarkar, Benoy K., *The Political Philosophies Since 1905*, Vol. II, 1942.

Seal, B.N., "Meaning of Race, Tribe, and Nation", in *Inter-Racial Problems*, edited by G. Spiller London, 1911.

Seal, B.N., *Positive Sciences of the Ancient Hindus*, Longmans, Green & Co., London, 1915.

Seal, B.N., *Presidential Address at the Opening Ceremony of Tagore's Visva Bharati, Shantiniketan*, 1921.

Seal, (Acharya) B.N., Letter to Tagore from Mysore, 1921.

Seal, B.N , *Report as Chairman of the Mysore Constitutional Reforms Committee*, 1922-23.

Seal, B.N., *Report as Chairman of Mysore Committee on State Aid to Industries*, 1924.

Seal, B.N., *Presidential Address at the Mythic Society*, Bangalore, 1924.

Seal, B.N., *Advent of Youth*, 1924.

Seal, B.N., *Rammohan—The Universal Man : Two Addresses at Bangalore (1924) and Calcutta (1933).*

Seal, (Sir) B.N., *Address on Sri Ram Krishna as the General President of the World Parliament of Religions*, Calcutta, 1936.

Seal, B.N., *Quest Eternal*, 1936.

Seal, (Acharya) B.N., *Reply to Birthday Felicitations*, Calcutta, 1938.

Seal, (Acharya) B.N., *Last Message*, Calcutta, 1938.

Seal, (Sir) B.N., Autobiography (Ms).

INDEX